# The New Normal
# Vol. II:

## More Tales from
## International School Teachers

CURATED BY MATT MINOR
AND KEVIN A. DUNCAN
on behalf of the
Children of Haiti Project

ISBN: 9781091961760

# DEDICATION

To Tom Duncan and Bob Minor, two men who taught us and many others that "the truly educated never graduate."

# STORY LOCATIONS

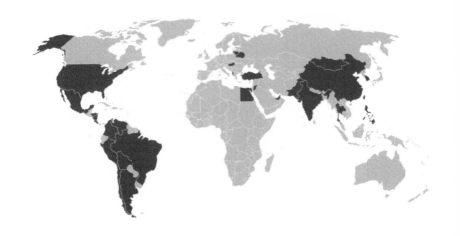

# TABLE OF CONTENTS

**FINAL THOUGHTS**

# INTRODUCTION

## OUTSIDE OF THE EIGHT TO THREE
*Kevin A. Duncan*

When I was a student, it was always a little jarring to see my teachers out and about in town. They actually eat at restaurants like other human beings? What are they doing wearing a t-shirt...and shorts? They don't just drink coffee all day and sit under fluorescent lights at school while coming up with homework assignments and group projects?

Even though I spent time with them every day and knew that my own life was much more than school, it was hard to grasp how human my teachers were. Despite my ignorance, they experienced the full gamut of emotions—pain, joy, sadness, pride, shame, laughter, etc.—as they grew their families, experienced tragedy, built relationships outside of work, tried and succeeded, tried and failed.

As my childhood teachers in Columbia, Tennessee were real human beings, so are the thousands of people who teach internationally at schools in countries big and small, developed and developing. This book offers a direct glimpse of those humans that get up every morning in countries they weren't born in to teach students how to multiply, play the flute, write fluently, think critically, and be world citizens. What follows are forty-one stories, most set outside of the 8:00 a.m. to 3:00 p.m. Monday-Friday school schedule. In these pages, the gamut of emotions is on display—laughter at a moment of culture shock, sadness in losing a loved one, thankfulness toward a good Samaritan, admiration for a person with so much compassion but so few possessions, fears both small and large—of stepping outside a foreign apartment building for the first time, or of a couple trying to raise an adopted child halfway across the world from their family.

Each tale provides several brushstrokes on a canvas that will, by the time you finish reading, represent the real lives of many teaching abroad. This collection will show how life for them isn't always about lesson plans, homework assignments, and tall cups of coffee. While some stories do take place within school walls, most occur in those "t-shirts and shorts" moments, times when the authors are known as Ken and Kathy or Jay and Dani, not "Mr." and "Ms." Those moments when people talk directly to each other instead of waiting for someone to raise their hand. Teachers spend so much of their time outside of a classroom's fluorescent lights, even if their students wouldn't fully recognize them in the natural light of day. Though the streets the authors walk down in rural Chile, urban China, and everywhere else in between might be more exotic than typical roads, the people who tell these stories are every bit as human as the next.

# THE TALES

# RAW MEAT & MIXED METAPHORS
*Nicole Gough*

In October of my second year living in Manila, some friends of mine decided to take advantage of our proximity to Mongolia and invited me to join them on a trip. Part of the appeal was spending a night in a traditional ger on the Mongolian steppe where we, along with our host family, would participate in household activities such as milking cows, collecting dung, and shooting things with a bow and arrow.

Thrilled to experience Mongolian culture firsthand, we signed up for a program that offered a two-hour information session that included a crash course in Mongolian language and customs we should learn and respect. We knew it was impossible to understand an entire culture in two hours, but we were excited to learn as much as we could about Mongolia's history and its cultural identity.

After 26 hours on a train from Beijing, we arrived at the office in Ulaanbaatar where we were shuffled into a little lobby whose walls were adorned with paintings of Genghis Khan and black and white photos of furry camels. A large man in a t-shirt and sweatpants rolled out from behind a computer and greeted us.

"Listen guys, I'm gonna get you out of here in less than two hours. You're only staying one night, ok? So you don't need the whole deal. I usually do a longer intro, but you're not staying long, ok? So this is Mongolian culture in a nutshell."

This he said in one breath, before I had time to take out my pen and information packet.

"There's the Sea World approach, ok, where you got the animals in cages. But this is open ocean, ok? Some nomads are dolphins and some are orcas. Mongolia is like an operating system, like Windows 95, ok? It's been reformatted."

We'd been sitting for one minute, and already I was a little confused. Caged sea animals and obsolete computer programs? Mongolian dolphins? Who was this man? He hadn't introduced himself. Nevertheless, six teachers make an eager and obliging audience, and so we all hastily scribbled notes.

Sea World, I wrote. Open ocean.

What little I learned about Mongolian culture from his lecture was buried beneath a pile of mixed metaphors and sudden topic shifts. One minute he was telling us about Mongolian history and its impact on present-day identity, and the next he was talking outer space.

"You know how to find a black hole?" he began at one point. Silence. Holly bravely ventured, "Gravity?"

"Well, yeah, but I'm talking about distortions, light, and matter," he went on.

Mongolia = black hole??? I scribbled.

Satisfied he'd conveyed enough cultural information, the man then enthusiastically guided us through a number of wild scenarios we might find ourselves in while exploring the Mongolian wilderness.

First, he assessed our equestrian skills. "Does anybody know the proper way to dismount a runaway horse? Anybody? No? Well I'll tell you how *not* to. Pulling the mane and choking the horse won't work. Do you know how many tiny bones are between the wrist and shoulder? A lot. 15. You're all experienced parachuters, right? You don't wanna do that. What you wanna do is an 11 o'clock roll, obviously. Not 12, not 10. Not here, not here, ok?"As my pen dashed erratically across the page, I began to panic. Was parachuting expertise a requirement for tourists hoping to visit the Mongolian steppe? Did this man frequently address groups of parachuting tourists?

Before I could ask, he then proceeded to describe how we'd launch ourselves off the horse safely. Afterwards, without a breath, he pointed to the painting of Genghis Khan on the wall. "See that guy right there? That guy rides a horse like a boss." He explained that if we were "fooling around" on a long hike and one of us fell over, we'd need to text Ulaanbaatar for first aid.

"You know how to tell if you cut a vein in your hand or just the meaty part? First, you cut off circulation in your arm. Then, hold your hand in the air. Find a rock and tape it to your palm. If it's bleeding all over, it's a vein. But you can avoid that. Just wear gloves."

After this, he thought hard for a second.

"Yeah, not too many animals around in the winter you need to worry about. Oh! PIT VIPERS! Watch out for crevices, they'll be full of pit vipers. But, you know, once you get bitten, you've got like five months."

Silence.

"…to *live?*" came Holly's voice.

The man stared.

"You might also see wolves, ok. You know what I do when I see a wolf? Throw my meat pack at it and take a selfie before it runs away."

Here I had to pause a little longer to understand why I'd be carrying a pack of meat with me out to the ger. A sleeping bag, I understood. Toiletries also made sense. But a separate bag stuffed with raw meat? I hadn't packed that.

After finishing that part of the lecture, the man scrutinized our wardrobe.

"Some of you are dressed okay right now. Some of you aren't."

He didn't elaborate on this any further, so we were left exchanging nervous glances and wondering which of us was dressed appropriately.

Finally, with a great bound, he was out of his chair and circling us.

"Ok, now it's time to go over how you enter the ger."

At this point, we were all trying very hard to listen to what he was saying, eager not to accidentally offend our Mongolian family, so I tried my best to take notes. We'd be staying with a former Mongolian wrestler, categorized as a dolphin in the man's open ocean analogy. The family would be somewhat modern, but we still had to respect the traditions.

The man told us that as the eldest, Carl would be responsible for entering the ger first and then introducing each of us in turn from oldest to youngest.

We were to enter the ger right foot first, with our packs in our left hands, and bow to the fire and our host. Tripping through the door frame was considered bad luck and made for an awful first impression.

If our host had his hands behind his back, we were not welcome to shake his hand. If he wanted to shake our hands, we could then remove our gloves and do so. If not, we could awkwardly stand in the ger with our winter clothes on.

Once we'd all filed into the ger, we would be seated. We were to only move in a clockwise motion once inside the ger. We were, under no circumstances, permitted to do the following:

- Point our feet toward the fire
- Walk between the two poles holding up the ger at the center
- Touch anyone's head or hat (both are sacred)
- Walk counterclockwise
- Touch items on the religious table
- Play with their funereal oil lamp
- Shake our hands to warm up (a sign of aggression)
- Roll up our sleeves (also a sign of aggression)
- Slouch when seated (a sign of weakness)
- Whistle (condemns someone in the ger to death)

Once we'd entered, they would have us sit down and serve us milk tea. Anything served to us, he explained, had to be consumed immediately. Afterward, they might leave us alone in the ger to rest. We weren't to interpret this as hostility.

Eventually, they'd return and serve us dinner, after which our host would pass around a bowl of airag, fermented mare's milk, and we would each take a sip.

"I'd bring antibacterial soap to rub on the rim," the man advised.

Next, they'd pass around a bowl of yogurt vodka, which sounded good to me. We would take a sip, and then each of us would individually be responsible for singing a song to the family. "Anything," he told us, "but 'Happy Birthday.' They called and asked us to tell people not to sing that one anymore, ok?" "Yeah, like they're hiking 20 kilometers to some random payphone in subzero temperatures to call this guy and tell people to stop singing Happy Birthday," Blair said later.

After the singing of songs, we'd drink more vodka and play games until what sounded like the wee morning hours. This I was on board with. I imagined the tense cultural differences melting away as we all bonded over traditional songs and vodka.

The man told us that we'd be taken to our own sleeping ger. If we wanted to help out with things around the house, we'd have to ask a few times, as Mongolian hospitality means treating guests like guests. (We'd have to beg to shovel dung, basically.) Begging to help with chores in exchange for home-cooked meals, long stories around a fire with our host family, and jolly singalongs seemed like an even trade to me.

"So that's it in a nutshell," he said, clapping his hands together. "You guys been keeping up with baseball? How about the Mets, huh?"

As the man slid away behind his computer, our Mongolian language teacher cautiously emerged from behind her own desk, a small woman with a serious face and a quiet demeanor every bit the antithesis of the man.

She guided Carl through his introductions and then taught us how to say things like, "I want to go back to Ulaanbaatar now" and "Hold your dog."

The next morning, we practiced our Mongolian the entire journey from Ulaanbaatar to the ox cart that would convey us to our ger on the steppe. Carl rehearsed his introductions at least a dozen times, and when we arrived at the ger, we carefully lined up in order of age.

As Carl introduced us with utmost solemnity, the host divided his strained attention between our faces and an old Western he was watching on TV. The six of us stood expectantly, careful not to move until we were instructed to.

While we fretted over whether our feet were too close to the fire or if we were slouching offensively, our ox cart driver entered the ger left-foot forward, moving counterclockwise before leaning up against the center poles with a cup of tea. He said something to our host, and both men turned to us and laughed.

The six of us were quickly moved into the sleeping ger, where we passed time counting the number of beams in the ceiling. The only time anyone came to check on us was at dinner, when a woman poked her head in, doled out six bowls of stew, and quickly darted back out.

To be fair, they *were* showing us a sort of reserved hospitality. They kept us fed and warm, and they even dug us a toilet a few meters away from our ger, but it was clear we were not invited to hang out with them in the main ger.

"It's like being in a low-security prison," Blair said.

At one point, Alicia went to the main ger to ask for a candle, and returned looking sad.

"They're having a party in there," she told us, as we looked up hopefully from our cots. Our evening's entertainment was Rosie reciting part of *Harry Potter* from memory until we all fell asleep. In the morning, the woman returned with breakfast.

"You go back to Ulaanbaatar now," she said, pointing outside toward the ox cart. As she closed the door, Holly shouted desperately in Mongolian, "Can we milk your goat?" The woman looked at us with a mixture of horror and pity.

To this day, Carl wonders if it was his introductions that landed us in solitary confinement. We think otherwise. A later comparison of our host with the photo of the Mongolian wrestler from our pamphlet revealed little resemblance.

"Maybe the wrestler died," Blair suggested later. "Maybe he was all about the exchange program and his family hates it, but they don't know how to get out of it."

We'll never know. There was a lot we would never know about Mongolia. We would never know the taste of fermented mare milk sipped from a communal bowl. We would never know the joy of sharing popular folk songs over gallons of straight vodka. We would never really get a sense of ger life or Mongolian farming.

But if you want to know about pit vipers, flesh wounds, or dismounting a runaway horse, I know six people who would be happy to share their notes.

In any case, I didn't need that raw meat pack.

*Nicole Gough, a native of Middletown, New Jersey, teaches in Manila, Philippines. She has taught high school English for 10 years, 2 in the U.S. and 8 in Egypt and the Philippines. You can read more of her adventures overseas on her blog lostamonglatitudes.com.*

# DRIVING LESSONS
*Anna Lisa VanHorn*

One evening in a Nicaraguan monsoonal rain, I found myself on a hill in rush-hour traffic, in the dark, with the frantic swishing of the wipers doing nothing to enhance my neverending view of brake lights. I sat rigidly, breathing deeply and praying I wouldn't stall or roll back into the line of cars behind me. The traffic light turned and, punching the clutch, I revved the gas and immediately killed the engine. With my foot firmly on the brake, I tried starting it again and again to the chorus of angry honks around me. I started shaking and in a panic looked at my friend Mike. He smiled and calmly told me to breathe. "You can do this, take your time," he said in Spanish. I took his advice, and sure enough, he was right. I did it.

I can only describe driving in Managua as a video game. It is terrifying. Aside from shifting gears, I now had to be on the lookout for people, chickens, speeding minivans, and the infamous unmarked speed bumps ("sleeping policemen," as Mike called them), not to mention other drivers.

I became the second driver of our shared 1996 Subaru. It was a rusted white station wagon that liked to announce its presence by honking at random intervals, whether driving on the street or at rest in a parking lot. Johanna and I drove that clunker of a car, with Quinn and Rhonda in tow, from beaches to volcanoes, from old colonial towns to the mountains and back again. The car would break down quite often, leaving the four of us on the side of the road imploring other drivers to help us. One good Samaritan nestled our battery in place with the t-shirt off his back. Another rode a bicycle for miles to retrieve a much-needed part after the brakes had gone out and we had miraculously glided to a safe stop in a gas station. Yet another group of strapping young men delivered a new fan belt as we waited roadside with smoke pouring from under the hood. Amazingly, after two years of driving the dilapidated Subaru, we resold it for exactly the same amount that we had paid for it, and then we dispersed to different locations around the globe.

I moved to Chennai, the third largest city in India. As one might imagine, Indian roads are definitely a more advanced level in the driving video game. Drivers share the road not only with the crush of other vehicles, but also with cows, horse-drawn carts, flower vendors, stray dogs, market stalls, coconut wagons, and pedestrians—lots of them. The painted white lines on the asphalt are merely a suggestion, as are many of the traffic signals. Motorbikes piled with families and belongings, three-wheeled tuk-tuks coughing up black smoke, taxis, SUVs, cars and giant tan buses with people dangling precariously out the doors all jockey for position on the narrow roads. Driving the streets of Chennai feels like being a small fish in an ocean food chain, constantly darting out of the way of the massive buses as they emerge from behind, sounding their long, low honks. Miraculously, the flow somehow works.

After a year of carpooling, getting rides in three-wheeled autos, and watching taxi drivers maneuver the streets Indian-style, I decided to buy a little Hyundai Santro to try myself. Both the school transport coordinator and the car dealer were a bit shocked when I asked to test drive the little silver car. "But what about your driver, madam?" they implored. "I am the driver," I replied, sliding into the right-side driver's seat with a nervous smile. It was a bit disorienting, my left hand gripping the stick shift in the center console, my right resting on the steering wheel. I pulled out on what felt to me like the wrong side of the road, taking one spin around the block slowly and cautiously, forcing myself to constantly remember that the "right" side is not actually "right." Turning back into the lot, I announced confidently, "I'll take it."

I drove that tiny box of a car all over southern India in the following years, often to the amazement of foreigners and locals alike. It steered me through intense moments, like the time I had to drive for blocks in reverse over piles of rocks and rebar down an increasingly narrow street, its reverse signal playing "Jingle Bells" loudly and repetitively. There were the gentle "love taps" the car and I gave to a few worn hawker carts sales carts and the occasional person while driving through the crowded backstreets (mercifully I never hit a holy cow). We outlasted the Chennai flood waters that, season after season, came higher than the car doors, rusting its wheel beds. We even experienced the sheer terror of driving in a typhoon with fallen trees blocking the streets, branches whipped up by powerful winds striking ominously against the Santro's metal frame. That car and I went through a lot. But, as anyone will tell you, all good things must come to an end. So after four years in Chennai, I sold the little silver car and moved across the world, yet again, to South America.

After six months of living in Lima, I finally had my residency card and thus could get my license. So at 5:00 a.m. on a grey and foggy morning, I was in the driver's side of a car at a beach-side practice course, preparing for my Peruvian driving test. The instructor sat in the passenger's seat and began barking commands at me in Spanish. When I looked at him blankly, he wagged his finger in front of my face, indicating I should start driving. I rolled down the window, calling out to my Peruvian friend Giova for help, and she began chasing the car while translating words like "blinker" and "steering wheel." I had to memorize two different courses, A and B, in a very precise order if I hoped to pass the test. The trickiest part was the parallel parking; it was to be done in one go, following a precise sequence of aligning, wheel turning, counting and (for some reason) only looking forward. During the practice, I accidentally glanced back over my shoulder, surprised to discover there was a *small child* sprawled out, eyes half open, lightly snoring in the backseat. Apparently, all of the turning and shouting hadn't awakened her. After a few more practice rounds, I was ready to "graduate" and try my skills on the official driving course.

Giova dropped me off with a hug and a "good luck." I took my place in the line of hopeful locals, many of whom had failed the notorious test multiple times. When a group of us were called to simultaneously pull in and out of our respective parking spots, the woman next to me suddenly jolted forward instead of reversing the car and slammed into a concrete block in front of the testing building. Needless to say, she didn't pass (even though she looked forward the whole time). Thankfully, I made it out of the contrived maze and after an hour of waiting, I was given a sheet of paper that I had to send to Giova with a question mark for translation. She replied with an excited, "You passed!!!"

To get to the next level, unofficially on Nicaraguan and Indian video game roads, or officially on a Peruvian test maze, I couldn't worry too much about unmarked speed bumps, a reverse signal that played "Jingle Bells," or a sleeping child in the back of a car. I didn't have to keep my eyes looking in any one specific direction. All I had to do was remember that it really is about the journey, not just the destination.

*Anna Lisa VanHorn was born in Waterloo, Iowa and raised in sunny San Diego, California. She has been an international teacher for her entire career, teaching third grade for 2 years in Managua, Nicaragua and second grade for 4 years in Chennai, India. She currently teaches fifth grade in Lima, Perú.*

# THE THINGS I CARRY
## *Kelsey Heeringa*

I have friends that moved from South Africa to China with an anvil. Others who crossed an ocean with a ladder they once found in a dumpster. As a minimalist who has packed and repacked for many moves, I often wonder if each of us, in any way, are a sum of the objects, especially the unnecessary ones, we choose to carry with us. For me, it's my brailler.

It's been an odd object to own everywhere I've been in the fifteen years since I worked at Perkins School for the Blind. This lunk of thick, gray metal is about the size of an old typewriter, has a foldable handle, and only nine keys. It weighs, in my professional opinion, approximately as much as a small elephant. I took it with me as proof to my deafblind student that I would stay within reach, and proceeded to haul it as a carry-on through airports all over the US, and eventually the world. I used it to braille him letters to share stories from my life. We brailled to plan our travels together, some real and some only imagined. We outlined parts of his memoir, a project we'd never complete because he died a few years later.

After that, I didn't keep the brailler for its brailling function anymore, but as a symbolic grip on that part of my identity. As it gathered dust on shelves or sat in overhead bins, it reminded me of the lens on life and humanity I'd learned by being known and loved by a few deafblind kids. It held in it a collection of hard-earned impressions about bravery and trust, communication against all odds, and the value of vulnerable one-on-one connection. Sure, I did some braille demonstrations in the occasional preschool class or to entertain my son's friends, but mostly I carried that damn brailler around the world because I was uncharacteristically attached to it, attached to the perspective of that time in life that I deeply wanted to hold onto. I wanted it to define me, and felt entrusted to remember and represent it in the world.

**********

It wasn't long after we'd unpacked the suitcases in Albania and plunked that beast of a brailler onto yet another shelf in another foreign land that I started to hear about Elizabeth. People I met described her with the taste of awe in their voice. "You'll love her," they kept saying. "She is a writer, like you. And...she *also* founded this project empowering the Roma in Kosovo, and she gives speeches in England, and has her own publishing company, and I think she's running in a 10K race this weekend to raise money for books for the kids she reads to on Tuesdays..." The list would go on and on, and everyone had allegedly *just* seen her but had no idea when she would be spotted again.

I wasn't sure I even believed in this Elizabeth, as if trying to encounter this British Wonder Woman/Mother Teresa/Mary Poppins was the traditional snipe hunt for new foreigners in town. I started to picture her as this small, elusive jungle creature with black fur, bettering the world by day and disappearing in the branches at night if I tried to get too close.

I eventually caught a glimpse of Elizabeth by going to hear her speak at an event. She had unembarrassed flickers of grey in her short hair and a ready smile, lit from within, right in the face of the troubled world. She spoke of the grassroots ways her community in Kosovo was working to turn poverty on its head. She told us about it like a storyteller would, not like a fundraiser. I started joining her on some of her projects in the city, moving at her speed, which felt like wading into a quiet, forceful river, a river of optimistic hard work, tall boots, and bulging canvas bags.

I looked at these bags one day as we walked, hanging like weights from her sides, and I wondered what exactly a woman like this carried with her in the daily current. I knew her computer was stuffed in there somewhere, image from *The Giving Tree* stuck onto the outside of it, containing the manuscript for her newest book. According to her self-imposed deadline, it was only days away from completion.

We passed a Roma woman begging on the street.

"I used to have some little treats leftover from a fundraiser to give to Roma children, but I think I've run out," she said, half peering into the black hole of one of the bags. On the surface, I could see some children's books, a bunch of leeks, and her trademark diary/calendar, stuffed chockablock full of notes and papers askew.

"Those are some serious bags you carry," I observed.

"Yes, well," she said, as if this was the whole explanation. Then she continued, "Once when I was on holiday, I found this beautiful rock in a riverbed. It was quite big, but it had these really lovely lines and I decided to keep it. Then I forgot about it

19

and didn't find it again until a week later! So in addition to everything else in here, I had been carrying around a giant rock for an entire week!"

I laughed unreasonably hard at this, enjoying the ways she was so much that I aspired to be and was also so imperfectly and wonderfully human. Moving ever-forward and doing her best, she sometimes didn't even remember exactly what she carried with her through her days. She did, however, seem confident in the knowledge that it all added up to fullness.

I kept this story of the rock the way she'd kept the rock itself: beauty tucked away like a treasure, ultimately serving as a surprising reminder that we try to hold tightly onto that which we feel is important, even if sometimes in a bumbling, awkward way. Occasionally we clutch things we needn't hold so tight, sometimes we lose things we never meant to; we thoughtfully fill our bags, forget, laugh at ourselves. We collect and refine what matters, what is worthy of our time and space, again and again.

*********

"So another project I'm doing is with the Society for the Blind in Kosovo," Elizabeth tells me one day over tea. "They're trying to raise enough money to teach the local blind kids to read and write in braille. They can't attend school until then, so many of them have already missed out on years of their education."

Of course she was somehow doing this, also. "Elizabeth. I used to work with deafblind kids. I *own* a brailler."

"You own a brailler?! Here in Albania?"

I instantly sensed that my years of lugging an $800 brailler around the world purely for sentimental reasons were coming to an end. A blind kid in Kosovo would need it much more than I ever did. Even considering this idea broke and filled my heart in more ways than I knew how to deal with at first. And yet, a few weeks later I was on my way to Kosovo, my brailler taking its final trip with me in the overhead bin of a bus.

With an hour to see the small city of Gjakova we stopped to admire the exterior of the Hadum mosque. The brailler drew its usual share of quizzical attention and after Elizabeth explained its purpose (in Albanian), the man in charge decided to unlock the door and lead us inside. Taking off our shoes, Elizabeth's mismatched socks reminded me of my deafblind student that I'd lost. As I walked around I wondered what he'd think of this place, and how far this brailler and I had journeyed in his absence. After a gracious welcome and tour, the man asked if I would braille a note in their guestbook. And while I thought I'd brailled for the last time the night before, there I found myself brailling a note of gratitude in a mosque in Kosovo, baffled at the ways life is often an unfolding so unlikely, and also so inescapable all in the same breath. Gratitude was of course the right bookend to this part of my story, in an obscure nook of the world, in an ancient place of worship so foreign to me but certainly no stranger to honoring things unseen.

Then onwards to meet the blind kids at the center where they'd just gained enough funding to teach braille to a few children for a couple months. The two teachers, one of them blind himself, moved eagerly and affectionately between the students, all at varying levels of ability but simultaneously unlocking this secret of literacy for the first time.

My brailler was slated to go home with a small nine-year-old girl, Besiana, who I found hammering out braille dots manually with a sharp tool. In this manner, it would take approximately forever to write a few sentences, not to mention that she'd have to do the whole thing backwards in order to read it forwards once she flipped the paper. She moved determinedly from one space to the next, grinning all the while. Her father told Elizabeth that Besiana had spent years asking why she couldn't go to school like her sister. He said he would do anything for her, that he would give her his eyes if he could.

Besiana flipped over the page to try and read it. Just a string of As and Bs so far, but she knew that together they spelled "baba," the Albanian word for dad. Her father looked on with the other parents, his face gripped with emotion.

I cried at the end of my day, as if a chapter in my life fifteen years ago was closing yet again. This kind of giving, giving that felt like it really cost me something, swelled inside with layers of gratitude, mourning, and a bottomless sense of interconnectedness. I knew I'd left a real piece of myself, and a piece of my deafblind students who had unknowingly changed me forever. From them, there is a sparking and dancing energy that Besiana can't yet know is thundering towards her, and as she grows, I hope it carries her into the world in mysterious ways, just as it has carried me.

*********

Weeks later, at a meeting of the writers' group we'd started, Elizabeth reached into one of those mysterious bags and pulled out an incredible rock. I laughed. "You're carrying *another* rock in your bag?"

"I picked this up on my trip to Jordan," she said. "And I brought it back here for you."

When she handed it to me, I marveled at the colors and reverently felt its weight in my palm. This she had carried *for me*. Every ounce of it felt like a gift, a reminder that what I carry and what I leave behind does not define me, but it does remind me. It reminds me about who I intend to be, and also occasionally serves as a way I leave an odd breadcrumb trail behind me in this lifetime. I'm amused to say I now carry with me this red and purple rock from a land I've never seen, and with it a vision of the type of person I aspire to be.

*Kelsey Heeringa, originally from Grand Rapids, Michigan, started adventuring at age 19 by taking a job at a school for deafblind students. A couple at-risk youth programs, organic farms, theatre productions, and summers in a tent later, she and her family finally ventured abroad. Since then, she's been writing, volunteering, or working in Communications alongside school communities in Tanzania, South Africa, Albania, and now China.*

# MENU, PLEASE
*Dave Archer*

After moving to Korea to begin my second international school teaching job, I decided the most practical thing to do was learn how to read and write the language, Hangul. In the country for about a week, I'd put in a few solid hours on my first Sunday writing the alphabet and pronouncing the syllables. I figured I had learned at least enough to sound out a few words on a lunch menu. In hindsight it is clear my confidence was premature, but I ventured out of my apartment for a bite to eat, hoping to navigate an authentic cultural experience.

I left my high-rise and set out looking for the perfect restaurant, avoiding the bustling streets near my apartment for a quieter neighborhood across the river. It being a Sunday afternoon, most places were empty or closed, so I had to do more sleuthing than usual. I walked for about thirty minutes, my hunger and apprehension increasing concurrently. Eventually I spotted a small restaurant with a friendly-looking emoji on the sign smiling at me, beckoning me inside. Through the window, a family seemed to be enjoying their lunch. I figured I ought to try this place out.

Stepping inside the restaurant yielded a reaction from the patrons and workers not unlike those from card players in an old saloon, when in blows a stranger from the storm. If a pianist had been present, the ragtime would have stopped, the good times replaced with stunned silence. If anyone had spoken English, they likely would have asked me if I was lost. I looked down at the floor, surprisingly not out of embarrassment, and noticed the shoes of all the people in the place, some on the floor and some on a shoe rack. I took the time to unlace my size-13 Nikes and find a spot for them, gaining an extra few seconds to formulate my next move, but the rack was clearly not built for my American kicks. By the time I stood back up, my forehead was sweating from nerves, and all eyes were still upon me.

No one moved as I tentatively stepped farther into the restaurant. There was no one else eating alone. With a false aura of confidence, I walked to a table as far from the family as I could, behind a beam that would conceal any further antics from view.

As a six-and-a-half-footer, the last place I would choose to eat a meal is on the floor. My legs don't cross comfortably, nor do I have the core strength to sit up with my legs out in front of me for very long. If I do find myself on a floor, I have to be perched back on my elbows for any sort of lasting comfort. This day, however, I did my best to cram my legs into a somewhat tolerable position to get me close enough to the table to hover over it.

Looking around the room, I saw nothing denoting what kind of food I might eat, nor did the kitchen smell provide any clues. I expected at least a menu written on the wall as I had seen in

25

some other restaurants. I did, however, happen to catch the eye of the curious-looking *ajumma*, the lone, elderly waitress. She held up one finger and raised her eyebrows in a questioning manner. I assumed she was asking if anyone would be joining me, so I returned the gesture of one finger back, adding a regretful smile and nod of my head.

In a few minutes she brought out a tray covered in bowls holding foods of varying colors and textures, which I came to realize were the side dishes to a meal I was going to receive, but hadn't ordered. I recognized a bowl of bean sprouts and another of cooked spinach. There looked to be a salad of spicy cucumbers, for any food in Korea blanketed in a red color is nine times out of ten going to be spicy. I had to try it, even though I knew, with my constitution, that there was a close to 100% chance I'd end up with heartburn.

Another bowl had strings of pickled radishes, and yet another contained something that looked like milk-chocolate-covered pretzels, which delighted me for a split second until it turned out to be some sort of root vegetable. I was skeptical of nearly everything, but this was lunch adventure time, and my biggest worry wasn't that I would eat something that would make me sick, but instead that I would offend someone in my new home country just because I was unfamiliar with their cuisine.

I picked my way through the multitude of side dishes, doing my best to keep a light grip on my metal chopsticks so my fingers wouldn't ache. Some of the foods were definitely a challenge to pick up. My dexterity would need to improve if I planned to live in Korea for long.

Ten minutes later the food I didn't order arrived at my table. Again it was served in bowls, but this time in two that were quite large. One bowl was friendly-looking, a heaping pile of white rice. The other caused my eyes to narrow in skeptical disbelief. It looked like ziti in marinara sauce. Had I stumbled into an

Italian-Korean fusion restaurant? In addition to the main course, the *ajumma* also presented me with a pair of gardening scissors. I was stumped. After staring at the ziti for awhile, I ascertained that I should just dump one bowl into the other and make a rice casserole of sorts, so I looked up in hopes of catching my server's eye again, only to realize that she had been watching me stare at my food the whole time and hadn't moved. Clearly she was expecting a good show.

My confusion clear as day, she knelt down across from me, picked up the shears, and began aggressively cutting and stirring into the ziti repeatedly. This is the part of lunch that made me want to lace up and head to Burger King, because the tentacles that began surfacing churned my stomach much in the way they churned within the spicy sauce. It was not an Italian fusion restaurant, but a spicy octopus restaurant, identified plainly on the sign by a friendly, smiling little octopus emoji that somehow hadn't looked so octopus-like twenty minutes earlier.

The sauce wasn't too spicy even for my weak esophagus. It being an octopus restaurant, I enjoyed the creature cooked to what I assume was perfection, as it wasn't chewy like I'd expected, and it was definitely dead enough not to try to crawl out of my mouth. The ziti-looking morsels were actually little rice cakes in pasta form, and they accompanied the flavors and textures of the rest of the dish really well. As I got down to the last bits of food in my oversized bowls, I opted for a spoon, as my chopsticking skills seemed to worsen as the meal went on.

I joined the Clean Plate Club, nearly licking the bowl, and leaned back on my elbows with a sigh of accomplishment and contentment. The *ajumma* came and collected my bowls, eyebrows raised in delight, and as she smiled she said something in Korean that I took to mean, "Congratulations, foreigner, I didn't think you had it in you."

*Dave Archer grew up in Beverly, Massachusetts, caught the travel bug early, and started adventuring in his teens. After discovering his love of teaching, he moved to Kuwait where he taught for three years. For the past seven years he has been teaching 5th grade in South Korea, and inching toward his goal of visiting a country for every letter of the alphabet.*

# TWO COUCHES
## *Matt Minor*

I come from a long line of men who are terrible at delivering bad news. My dad is especially subpar, having just one month earlier told me of his terminal, Stage 4 stomach cancer before immediately asking, "Did you end up getting that new position you applied for?"

The weeks after that conversation had been a whirlwind of flights back and forth between South America and Orlando. I was living in the mountains of Medellín, Colombia, a city yet to shake its notoriety for cocaine exportation in spite of the fact that it had recently been chosen as the world's most innovative city. Colombia was a long way from Dad, so when a friend mentioned that cycling was a great way to keep one's mind occupied, I was desperate for the distraction.

An hour of preparation, including adjusting the bike seat to optimize my stride, squeezing into a painted-on cycling outfit, and dabbing Vaseline between my toes to lessen friction, helped me look the part of a cyclist. Not the lean-and-chiseled kind, but rather the former-athlete-looking-to-find-his-abs-again kind. I pedaled around the parking lot for five minutes, making sure I felt balanced and able to clip my shoes in and out of the pedals with ease. "Don't worry if you end up falling over," Jay reassured me, "it happens to rookies when they stop at a light and forget they're attached to their bike."

We descended toward a winding road that would lead us to the main route up the mountain, a climb famous amongst the local cycling crowd and a Mecca for out-of-town riders. Three minutes into the ride, we encountered a construction zone where traffic began crawling. Jackhammers pounded into the asphalt, and car horns honked like threatened geese as we cautiously merged into a single lane, bullied by the larger vehicles clamoring for their place in line. As I hugged the right side of the lane, a large object appeared in my peripheral vision. Instinctively, I veered away from the SUV's side mirror, causing my front tire to slide off the three-inch ledge separating the raised new road from the old dug-up section. My sweaty hands clamped on the brakes, and my right leg attempted to stretch itself out to catch my fall. Forgetting that my right leg was clipped into the bike, I propelled myself harder towards the ground. Bracing for impact, my left shoe twisted out of the pedal, freeing my left leg from the bike. I turned my head to avoid hitting the ground just in time to see my leg under the tire of the SUV. In the three seconds I pondered the lack of pain, the adrenaline wore off. An intense burn shot through like a lightning strike to the ankle.

Traffic behind me stopped, braking automatically for yet another obstacle on the road. The few construction worker witnesses assumed the SUV had run over my bike and that I had merely twisted my ankle, in spite of the tire marks now tattooed across my calf. Knowing that there was likely a break, I scooted across the lane of traffic on my butt like a dog on the living room carpet. Jay turned around, having missed the action, assuming I had just somehow rolled my ankle during the fall.

"Down already?" Jay asked half-teasingly.

"Ummm, the wheel...went over...my leg," I stated robotically.

"Aw man, that sucks. I guess that ankle will be too swollen for you to ride back. Hold on, this lady is yelling at me in Spanish. Let me see what she wants."

Jay walked over to the SUV and shakily conversed with the driver. In spite of having lived in Honduras and Colombia for a combined four years, Jay's spoken Spanish often left the listener leaning in with that slight turn of the head you give a toddler when they're speaking. The driver's intention was to check on my well-being, but as she smiled, waved, and drove off, it was clear that there was some confusion about my condition.

As Jay returned to check on me, I felt lightheaded and lay down to avoid fainting. "I can't believe the wheel of that SUV ran over my leg," I muttered, willing myself not to vomit.

Silence.

"Wait—the wheel of the SUV? Are you SERIOUS?" I had never heard such impressive inflection in Jay's voice. If only he could apply that when he asked questions in Spanish. "I thought you meant the wheel of your BIKE! I just told the driver that you were fine and that she didn't need to stay! We need to get you to a hospital NOW!"

Jay quickly hailed a taxi for me, and we met at the hospital a few minutes later. After handing over my Colombian ID and insurance card, Jay turned to find me in my skin-tight cycling suit being prayed over by a nun. I was Richard Simmons in "Sweatin' to the Oldies," being exorcised. This made me very uncomfortable for more reasons than just my outfit. I had a twelve-year history with nuns from Catholic school and my quota was filled. I thanked her in Spanish while attempting to pawn her off on a patient who wasn't a recovering Catholic.

The emergency room was clean and efficient, with nurses attending to my every need. They even managed to find an English-speaking surgeon who reassured us that the swelling would go down in time for the next morning's surgery. He would need to repair a broken fibula and ankle, and I would be gaining some hardware in the form of a steel plate and five screws. I could now set off metal detectors at airports around the world.

After a successful surgery and hospital visits from my friends, it was time to head home. My wife Cailin helped me get settled on our living room couch which would be my recovery spot for the next six weeks. My principal and colleagues urged me not to worry about my fifth grade students: they would be in great hands with a trusted teacher's assistant.

After calling Mom and proceeding from shock to sympathy to shared laughter about how often I find myself in story-worthy moments, I placed my next call to Dad in Florida. He was always calm, the kind of dad to whom you would admit denting the car, knowing his first reaction would be to ask if you were okay. I pulled up his Skype number and, as it rang, tears clouded my eyes. I choked up at the reality of the situation. Not my reality of being stuck on a couch for a few frustrating weeks, unable to work or travel, but Dad's reality of being stuck on a couch 1,500 miles away, never to work or travel again. I was healing; he was dying.

With tears still wet on my face, I heard Dad pick up on the other end. Excited to hear from me, he immediately asked about my weekend. Staying true to my inherited male tendencies, I clumsily attempted to downplay my situation. "We went to this new Thai restaurant that just opened down the street, and it was pretty good. Then yesterday I went for a bike ride, and well, ha ha, I got into a bike accident and had surgery this morning. What about you? What did you get up to this weekend?"

Over the next six weeks, Dad and I spent hours each day talking on Skype. We joked about our frail bodies and the guilt we felt relying on our spouses to take care of us. Keeping true to our Midwestern roots, we reported on the weather in our respective locations and expressed our pleasure in not having snow to shovel. A Monday morning Super Bowl recap left us marvelling at how Tom Brady could pull off another last minute comeback win. Dad laughed as I recalled seeing my favorite nun during physical therapy at the hospital. He reminisced about the hours spent at the baseball field watching my brother and me during our childhood years.

As the weeks passed, physical therapy and a lot of rest brought me closer to walking again. Meanwhile, Dad's cancer continued to spread, and I began noticing that he was mentally sharp in the mornings but fading by the afternoons. He sometimes slurred words due to a lack of oxygen to his brain. Every few days he would get confused as he spoke, often repeating the same thing from a few minutes before.

My last clear conversation with Dad took place the day after Valentine's Day. He jokingly asked if I had taken my wife out for a romantic dinner in the city. I recounted crutching a quarter of a mile down the street while Cailin was napping, in order to to surprise her with flowers. We laughed as I told him how I had misjudged my ability to lug the flowers back in the undersized bag I had taken. Dad praised me for piecing together enough Spanish to convince the flower shop employee to deliver the bouquet at the end of her shift. Calling out to my stepmother Linda, he retold the entire story with enthusiasm in his voice. She bragged how Dad had secretly called their local florist that same day and ordered her favorite flowers, coordinating with a friend to deliver them to the house. Like father, like son.

It was his final act of kindness.

Soon Dad could no longer piece together sentences. His voice grew raspier. It was more difficult for him to push out any words. Even the early morning conversations, when he had previously sounded his clearest, were gone. I called him frequently, telling him how much I loved him, quietly hoping for a rally or a small moment when Dad would "reappear." It never came.

Roughly three months to the day after he was given his diagnosis, Dad passed peacefully while holding Linda's hand. He was surrounded by family and friends throughout his time in hospice. Although I wasn't able to be with him physically, our Skype conversations and stories from the couch kept us connected along the way.

My untimely accident gave me an unlikely gift: the gift of time. Time to call Dad in the morning when his brain was fresh. Time for memorable moments and daily conversations. Time for laughter and tears. Time on the couch that forced me to face a reality I didn't want to acknowledge. I am thankful for the many moments I had with Dad in the first 37 years of my life, but I am especially grateful for the time we spent on our respective couches, healing and dying together for those last eight weeks of his life.

*Matt Minor, a native of Chicago (Elgin), Illinois, teaches in Shanghai, China. He has taught in elementary schools for 19 years, 8 in the US and 11 in South Korea, Thailand, Colombia, and China.*

# AMERICA: *MY* OVERSEAS
## *Audrey A. Enriquez*

*"You look so Asian today. You know you need to look professional in western business attire here, right?"*

I had just entered the faculty room, having finished my first class on the first day after spring break, feeling beautiful and happy with the way the class had gone. My department head was seated at the table; I looked at him in surprise after he spoke. But he was no longer looking at me.

*"You look so Asian today."*

But I **am** Asian.

*"You know you need to look professional in western business attire here, right?"*

But I **am** professional.

Really though, I was used to having my professionalism questioned based on my appearance and background.

*"Wait...you're from the Philippines? But you speak such good English!"*

I'm a Third Culture Kid: born in the Philippines, raised in Indonesia. English is my first language (Bahasa Indonesia my second, and Tagalog or Filipino my third). My childhood friends were from Germany, Malaysia, and New Zealand, and we spoke in English. My favourite teachers were from Canada and Scotland. I learnt British spelling and words (colour and queue, not color and line), played football (not soccer), and began counting "one" with my thumb (not my forefinger). I earned a 7 out of 7 in IB English and have a Master of Arts in Teaching English. So, yes—I speak "good English."

It was with such "good English" that I had begun my overseas teaching career in an international school in New York City. I was excited to be with students and colleagues not just from America, but from Australia, Brazil, Canada, Colombia, England, Hong Kong, India, Japan, South Korea, Italy, France, the Netherlands, Jamaica, Saudi Arabia, and Taiwan as well. It would be a return to that comfortable connection of my childhood amongst global citizens, a tribe of travelers, creators of a common third culture, seekers of a home away from home. I would be happily welcomed and embraced for my differences. I would, again, be part of a diverse and open family.

Or so I had thought.

My dear friend—also an international school teacher—had recently gifted me with a beautiful maroon and gold Indian kurta when she came to visit from Mumbai during Spring Break. She intentionally sought to give me something unique and local, and meticulously chose the kurta for its vibrant colour and intricate detail. It was carefully wrapped in tissue paper and presented with love. As I unfolded the kurta and listened to the story of the lengths she had gone to procure it, I vowed to wear it often and with pride. The kurta was, after all, a symbol of our long friendship across many homes and cultures.

Earlier in the morning, I had taken great pains in making sure my jewelry and shoes did not distract from the simple beauty of the kurta. I had smoothed the wrinkles from the long top, making sure it hung the length of my arms and well below my knees, as I tightened the ribbon around the trousers that hugged my legs tightly. I had protected my precious outfit against the subway elements under a light coat. I had felt comfortable and confident as I entered the school.

So what does *looking Asian* and not wearing *western business attire* have to do with my teaching?

Shocked at my department head's comment, I left the room and stepped outside for a breath of fresh air. I wanted to march right back into the faculty room and throw my question at him. But I had to let the urge go because I had more classes to teach.

I ducked into the bathroom once I got back inside to make sure I looked all right. I dabbed a couple of cold paper towels on my face, and looked into the mirror above the sink. I noticed the full-length mirror behind me, then slowly turned around. The light was bouncing off the gold inlay. I walked forward and the light started dancing around. I reached up and the same light caught the edge of my sleeve. I moved my hand back and forth, mesmerised by the flashes. I began to make intricate hand movements, following the paths of light emitted by the gold inlay. I took a step back and noticed the maroon then, deep and dark, with swirls emerging as I kept taking small steps back. I stopped moving and took a long, good look at my kurta. It was absolutely beautiful. I looked up, and saw myself. I was absolutely beautiful, too.

I wore that Indian kurta once a month for the rest of the year. That, and the indigo and silver Thai silk sarong my sister-in-law got me from Bangkok. I felt—and was—beautiful and proud, comfortable and confident, each and every time.

I am the English teacher who rocks her Indian kurtas and Thai silk sarongs.

And now, I have added to my ensemble pieces of America to honour my new home: a custom-made solitary opal ring from New Mexico; a one-of-a-kind pair of turquoise earrings from Texas; a unique solid silver necklace from Florida; an antique amber bracelet from New York. I take these pieces from the West and frequently blend them boldly with my Asian dress. This is my business attire—one example of the amalgamations of who I am, how I live, and how I teach.

*Audrey A. Enriquez, a native of Manila, Philippines, teaches in Basking Ridge, New Jersey. She has taught middle and high school English for 22 years, 11 in the Philippines, 10 in New York, and 1 in New Jersey.*

# HAIRCUTS
## *Jason D. Mott*

When talking with friends and family about living abroad, they always assume that the most difficult aspects of living in a foreign country are the obvious: the language, the food, and the distance from family and friends. These things are important and they can be difficult, but people tend to be ready for those challenges. They come in waves of frustration or homesickness, but they are also part of the beauty of the experience. You make new friends, you learn a new language. You start to love trying new cuisines. Surprisingly, the most difficult aspects of living outside of my home country are the small things—the things that you would never think of. The tiny daily annoyances that can build up to be nearly unbearable. Everyone has that little nuisance. Mine is getting a haircut.

From birth until the age of 22, I went to the same barber. Her name is Valerie and somehow, when I see her this summer, she will look exactly the same as she did when I was five. It might have something to do with all of the chemical preservatives floating around an old barbershop, but Valerie is timeless. And so is her barbershop. It is the kind of place that still has the red and white striped pole slowly twirling outside. There is a sign on the door that says "Walk-ins Welcome." A good haircut still costs $14 at the Village Barber, and no matter who else is in the barbershop, they will inevitably ask where I work. Upon hearing that I teach internationally, they will know exactly who I am and who my father is. To be honest, I love it.

As much as visiting the Village Barber fills me with nostalgic joy, I still hate getting my hair cut. I find it to be a tedious task that must be done. I went to the same place for my entire life because I didn't have to tell anyone how to cut my hair; Valerie already knew. When I went away to college, I would visit my family often enough that I always went back to the Village Barber. When I got my first teaching job in small-town Iowa, I was lonely and would still drive to visit my parents frequently. So I just went back to the Village Barber. But when I moved to a new school that was far from my hometown and started to put down some roots, I had to find another solution. This is when my haircut troubles began.

I bounced around a few different barbers in the last few years I lived in the US. I couldn't seem to hold down a steady hair routine. Every time I went to a new place, I had to explain how I wanted my hair to look, made the same awkward small talk, and hoped that everything turned out right. These interim barbers could never fully grasp how to best cut my hair, who I was, nor who Papa Mott was. And then something happened that I wasn't planning for: I met my wife. She convinced me to attend the Iowa international teaching job fair; before I could remember the clipper number that was best for the sides of my head, I was stepping off the plane in Shanghai, China.

Adjusting to life in China was just as turbulent as one might imagine. But we overcame these initial frustrations and slowly started to adapt to the big challenges of living in a new country. It was when my wife uttered those dreadful words that I knew I was going to meet my first major defeat. "Looks like it's time for a haircut." My stomach sank. I knew this was going to be a horrific experience.

My first idea was to ask a friend where he went for a trim. I ended up at a place called "Babyface." Men's cuts cost 180 RMB there, about $30 USD. I imagine that this is not actually that much money for a haircut, but it was still about double what I had ever paid before. And it took 90 minutes. The longest haircut I previously had endured was 13 minutes.

The first part of the experience was a hair wash. Nobody had ever washed my hair before, excluding myself and my mother when I was a toddler. The initial wash was accompanied by roughly 10 minutes of head massaging before moving onto the actual cutting of the hair. Normally this is done with clippers, but my Chinese barber was a professional and nothing less than a tiny pair of children's scissors would do for him. Fifty minutes later, my hair was slightly shorter than when I walked in, a difference even Sherlock Holmes might have missed. After the trim, I had a second hair wash, this one lasting even longer than the first. Then, it was time for the grand finale: the ear cleaning. This is a popular activity in China, and my barber went to it with the full gusto of someone who believed that his mission in life was to eliminate the waxy scourge plaguing my inner ears. I had no idea that it was possible to get that much Q-Tip inside of one's head. After the 90 minute "experience," I left Babyface struggling to decide whether or not I could make it an entire academic school year before getting my haircut again and whether the Q-tip treatment had left me partially deaf.

Later in the week, I was on my school's soccer field watching our student body load the buses to head home. I stood next to my principal, telling him about my dramatic haircut from the previous weekend. He told me that he got his hair cut in a dumpy little place right near school for 10 RMB (around $1.50). I was flabbergasted. How could I rationalize 180 RMB when I could accomplish this task for a fraction of the sum? Would a haircut this inexpensive include the Q-tip treatment? Would this mysterious barber speak English? I made a mental note to give this new barbershop a try.

I stood at a dirty alleyway, by another rotating red and white barber pole, trying to work up the courage to walk into what looked like someone's home. This was a local joint, a place that only Chinese people went—not someone from Davenport, Iowa. I finally walked into the barbershop, a cracked mirror on the wall and hair from the past week or so still on the floor, and engaged in a short conversation that was mostly me telling a man, in Chinese, that "I do not speak any Chinese." What transpired next was the beginning of four years of haircut bliss. It was a lesson for me in the benefits of true immersion into the local culture.

Each time I entered the barbershop the only other people there besides me was an old Chinese woman in one of those crazy space-looking helmets and my barber who smoked a cigarette nearby. He rarely spoke. He never asked me how I wanted my haircut. He just did it. Was it always what I wanted? No. Did I care? Not really. He used a pair of clippers to do most of the job and did about a minute and a half of scissor work on the top of my head. He shaved the back of my neck with a straight razor that looked like it was purchased brand new by the barber's grandfather and hadn't been sharpened since. The whole process took about five minutes. As I progressed in my Chinese, I started answering my barber's and the other regulars' questions about myself: I was a teacher who worked at the school next door; yes, that blonde lady there is my wife; no, we don't have any children. Although that was the extent of the questions, I was always happy to answer them. He was always glad to see me walk in and seated me right away.

As my time in Shanghai came to a close, I thought about how much I would miss those cheap haircuts. When I walked out for the final time, I thought about how unwilling I had been to take that first step into his barbershop, and how in the end it had been such an authentic way to experience local culture. Now I am living in Dubai and have gone back to a new English-speaking barber every time I get my haircut. And every time that I do get my haircut, I think back to the cramped confines of my Shanghai barbershop, the feel of the rusty straight edge razor sliding down my neck, and remember an amazing barber whose name I'll never know.

*Jason D. Mott, a native of Davenport, Iowa, is currently teaching music in Dubai, United Arab Emirates. He has taught for 3 years in Iowa, and 6 years in China and United Arab Emirates.*

# SANTA ARTURO
*Michelle Crosbie*

It took me a while to get it.

My family and I moved to Chile for so many reasons. We wanted our sons to learn Spanish. We wanted them to grow up to be kind and fair multicultural citizens. We wanted them to study with students from all over the world. We wanted to be somewhere safe and beautiful. We wanted to ski, to climb mountains, to see glaciers, deserts, Patagonia. We wanted to drink copious amounts of excellent Chilean wine. Mind you, those are all good reasons.

But, my story is about Arturo who, as it turns out, was the best reason to move to Chile.

When we first arrived at Nido de Aguilas, my sons were young enough to participate in the annual elementary Christmas show. The show was your run-of-the-mill elementary cute. There were

the perfunctory off-key songs energetically shouted, as opposed
to sung, by the colorfully-costumed youngsters; there was what
might be called dancing, and then there was Santa. I learned,
during our first year in the southern cone that Santa arrived on a
beautiful brown horse draped with crimson-colored cloth,
speaking only Spanish. In Chile, Santa arrived sounding a lot like
the janitor who cleaned my room every day.

I'll admit to being a little underwhelmed at first.

When I realized that Santa was actually Arturo, my first thought
was that the school had really saved some bank on this particular
feature of the show. Arturo had been a janitor at Nido (and still
is) for more than fifty years. He is also a Huaso, a Chilean
cowboy. This means that after work, after he cleans and
vacuums and moves heavy furniture around and helps just about
everyone else do what they need to do, Arturo goes up into the
hills behind our school and does what *he* likes to do. What
Arturo likes to do is to ride horses. In this space and time,
between the end of one work day and the beginning of the next,
Arturo truly lives. He has endless energy when he is in the
mountains; there, he is as free and unencumbered as any
American cowboy ever was. This *Huaso* tradition, embodied so
nobly in Arturo, is an incredibly important element of Chilean
culture often unnoticed by international teachers. At Christmas
time, Arturo blends his school life and his Huaso culture by
becoming Santa for the elementary students.

At school, however, Arturo is generally a much more
recognizable form of mortal, and his appearance is always
accompanied by the jangling wheels of his cleaning cart.

Many are the days when Arturo comes to my class after school
to clean my room. On most of these days, I am behind my
computer. I am reading and responding to emails; I am grading
papers. And, often on these days when I am busy at my
computer, Arturo will begin to talk. He is an avid and

enthusiastic storyteller, and because he claims more than a half century at the school—Arturo began to work at Nido at the age of sixteen—he has unlimited stories to tell. He has stories about the grandparents of our current students, stories of students whom he had to rescue from natural hazards like earthquakes and unforeseen snowfalls, and stories of the school during the Pinochet dictatorship. He has seen countless administrators, heads of school, teachers, parents, and students come through our school. Without having had any formal education himself, he is the heart of our school. Returning students come back to see him, and he remembers them all, and their parents, and their grandparents.

And I...I smile at Arturo, and I listen to him. Occasionally I even venture a question or two. But I almost never give him my full attention because I am always so busy with other tasks. In an age where no one has any time, Arturo does. He is never in a hurry. He is never too busy to talk or to help. Whenever I ask Arturo to do anything, he responds with a genuine enthusiasm. He is driven by a desire to help others and it is from that desire that he derives his happiness.

He tells me about the Chilean rodeos at the *media luna* behind the school. He tells me about the *Quasimodos*, the beautiful ceremony around Easter in which the Huasos decorate their horses and parade them through the Stations of the Cross in town. He invites me to share in these traditions; only occasionally do I take him up on his offer because his invitations fall outside of the kind of 'sexy' experiences most expats tend to seek out. He tells me all kinds of things that initially I was too busy and distracted to pay much attention to.

And so it went for the first couple of years we lived in Chile. And then: February 27, 2010. An 8.8 earthquake at approximately 3:30 in the morning. 200 seconds of holding my husband's hand in bed, of listening to glasses fall off shelves, of feeling the earth shift under our feet, of wondering, futilely, how to protect our young boys on the second floor.

We eventually rose to survey the new world wrought by this event. Bereft of power, we would learn more about the damage of the quake from our friends and family who phoned us than we could discover on our own. The damage was massive. School would be closed for a week, but teachers were asked to come in on Monday morning.

When I arrived, unsure of what state the school would be in, there was Arturo. He stood outside my room like a sentinel. He looked almost apologetic. He had come to my room—to all of our rooms—over the weekend to try to mitigate the disaster, to right the plants, to put the books back on the shelves, to clean up glass and debris, fallen furniture, and light fixtures. The wall clock had plummeted to the floor at precisely the time the earthquake struck. Arturo picked it up, put in new batteries, and time started again. This time, *I* began the conversation. I had questions; I had fears.

But Arturo had answers and assurances and history. "Ay Miss..." he began, and laughingly recounted the story of an even bigger earthquake he had endured and helped others through. I now lived in a country where, without any warning, the ground could tremble and moan and shift beneath my feet. But I had Arturo, my own piece of bedrock on which to lean.

Chile is indeed a gorgeous country with deserts and mountains, Patagonia, and Easter Island. It offers all of the opportunities we sought, and more. And yes, the wine, the wine is plentiful and delicious, but coming to know Arturo has taught me to forego some of the glitz and glamour of expat life. I have discovered that the richest experiences come when I simply slow down to listen and share time with the humble and kind Chileans with whom I work every day.

Santa looks different when you're abroad. Sometimes he wears cowboy clothing and arrives on a horse. Santa sounds different too. Instead of the expected jingle bells, Santa can announce his presence with the jangling wheels of his cart, a cart pushed daily, uncomplainingly, and with infinite patience. The day I fell in love with Chile was the day I understood that here Santa is a selfless janitor whose abundant bag is full of the most precious of all gifts: unending everyday kindness and the best and most genuine example of the culture my family and I left the States to experience.

*Michelle Crosbie, a native of New York, is the English department head in Santiago, Chile. She has taught in Chile for 12 years. Before Chile, Michelle taught in Florida, Venezuela, and Costa Rica where she met her wonderful husband Garrett and very dear friend and inspiration, Maureen McCann.*

# BRINGING KIDS INTO THE MIX...ABROAD
## *Dave Wood*

"I'm sorry, but I don't believe you signed up for an appointment," I said to the cute blond standing outside of my classroom.

It was approximately 2 p.m. on a Friday in early April, 2014. There was about an hour left in the latest round of parent-teacher conferences. Teachers were tired. Parents were scurrying around, trying to get every last minute question in about their children's growth, grades, and behavior. I was feeling a bit snarky and sarcastic.

My wife Jamie stood there in the doorway with a look of giddiness on her face. My previous comment didn't phase her one bit. At first I thought this was just the byproduct of ten years of marriage and her learning not to react to my quips. A second later, without her saying a word, I figured it out...

"No way!" I exclaimed.
"Check your email," she told me, trying not to burst out of her skin with excitement.

Thankfully, I was on a break between conferences, so I had time to open the link and read the adoption referral for the most beautiful five-month old girl. I must have stared at those four pictures for a good five minutes straight. They were really nothing more than pictures of her face, an angel smiling yet confused, an expression that communicated "why is someone taking my picture?" Jamie and I hugged repeatedly. My mind was racing, its thoughts vacillating between "Wow, we're going to be parents!" and "Holy crap, we have to be in the Marshall Islands in two and a half weeks—there's so much to get in order here!"

The rest of that afternoon was a blur. My final three conferences were probably the least productive ones I've ever had. All I remember is that during one of them, I interrupted the parent mid-sentence and asked "Do you want to see a picture of my daughter?" It's been over four years since that transformative hour and I still can't put into words how I felt. We'd been trying to adopt for almost five years, had recently changed adoption agencies, and had moved from Seoul to Shanghai. To see that journey come to a joyous conclusion so quickly was, well, indescribable.

I'm not sure how we did it, but we were able to gather all of the necessary paperwork, arrange for substitute teachers, book flights, and make all of the other arrangements in the 17 days that followed. (Admittedly, I was a bit jealous of those who get nine months to prepare for the arrival of a baby at this point!) In the midst of this whirlwind of preparation, I had to take my soccer team to Hong Kong for four days for a season-ending tournament. Rather than prepping for our next game, I was checking emails for last minute information from our agency and trying to book our flights. It was crazy, but all the logistics got taken care of and we were shortly on a plane headed to Majuro, a dot in the middle of the Pacific Ocean, to meet and pick up our daughter.

Yet, this whole time, when life slowed down and I could just sit and think, my thoughts almost always came back to one question—what's this going to be like without our families and friends from back home? In our "pre-international" lives, we envisioned raising our children near our families in the midwestern US. They'd go to the local schools. Grandparents would come watch their ballet recitals. We'd get together for birthday parties. Living 7,000 miles away from our nearest family member shattered that idea. At night, I started to think about what it would be like to grow our family in a way we never imagined. The prospects of adding a new addition to our family after 10 years of being just the two of us was daunting in and of itself. Doing so abroad, away from the comforts of the US *could* have been down right horrifying. But it wasn't. It had a lot of benefits we never imagined. Our school community became our support system overseas without replacing the one we had in place in the States.

What amazed me was the number of people, especially those with young children, we started talking to once we brought Kaida, our new daughter, home to Shanghai. Prior to this, we never really talked to this crowd because, frankly, we didn't have young children in common. Now, we were warmly welcomed by an entirely new community. Kaida very quickly became part of a playgroup and a member of the infamous "SRC stroller gang." (The SRC is the local compound where many faculty live.) They brought meals to us, told us the best way to get diapers in China, and taught us tricks for how to get all of our formula back from the States plus all the other little kiddie life hacks we needed to know. They became the people that I could vent to after suffering the umpteenth night in a row of less than four hours of sleep. They understood what it was like raising a child abroad;

I don't know how we would have gotten through that first year without them.

Yet, at the same time, they did not replace our families back home. Having a granddaughter was what finally got my parents, after five years of procrastinating, to figure out how to hook up their computer's webcam. This allowed Kaida to actually recognize them the first time we saw them nine weeks later at O'Hare Airport. Yes, they spoiled her rotten that first summer we were back and yes, they were sad when we went back to Shanghai. But rather than being jealous of the fact that our international school community could watch Kaida (and later, her younger sister Khloe) grow up in front of them, my parents came to profoundly appreciate the fact that we had such a supportive community abroad. Admittedly, weekly Skype dates definitely helped ease their sadness.

To this day, I don't know how many conversations my administrators had with "concerned" parents about my paternity leave during the three weeks prior to the AP US History exam. I know concerns were expressed, but my principals were incredible in how they protected me from that. (As an aside, that group scored the highest of any of my classes in six years of teaching APUSH. Perhaps the College Board should advise all AP teachers to just skip the last few weeks prior to their exam!) Every time I asked "Who's going to sub for me?" the response was "Don't worry about it. We'll take care of it."

Figuring out how to get our daughter back to China was another massive issue. I had to fly to Pohnpei, Micronesia to get a Chinese visa for Kaida because it was the only consulate in that part of the world that would do it. The hardest part was leaving my wife and new daughter behind in Majuro for a few days while I took care of this. Thankfully, our school's HR department expressed nothing but excitement and calm whenever we brought up a concern, helping us obtain the necessary paperwork quickly to get Kaida her visa. When similar challenges arose when we adopted our youngest daughter, Khloe, they were on the phone guiding us through the visa process, again.

We had been told when we went abroad that our school had a vested interest in our happiness, more so than an employer would in the States. Our adoption experience only confirmed that claim. We found our school to be profoundly supportive of us personally, not just professionally.

At the time that I'm writing this, Kaida is five years old. Although I was initially apprehensive about living in a gated community next to many people I see at work every day, I found that my children's play community was always right there. Kaida is fluent in Mandarin. I know maybe 25 words in Chinese, and that's on a 美好的一天 (good day)! One time someone shot me a dirty look and said something I didn't understand. When I asked Kaida what he said, she replied "You don't want to know!" To date, Kaida has already visited over twenty countries—she loved the beach in the Philippines, but not the scary monkey in Japan that hissed at her. Her age can be counted on one hand, but she's growing up with experiences that rival my seven hands' worth of years.

"But what about all of the opportunities she'd have in the US, like swimming lessons, soccer, and ballet?" I hear this frequently when we're back home in Minnesota and Wisconsin. However, Kaida does all of those things in China, and in fact, does most of them within a five minute walk from our apartment! We understand that with kids, our lives are lived in a bubble. We're just fortunate that we really like our bubble. There are way more benefits than we could have ever imagined.

There are hard things about raising a child abroad. She experiences close friends moving away far more frequently than I did growing up in Wisconsin. Of the original "Stroller Gang," she'll be the only one left next year as families will have moved on to Turkey, Ghana, and Chile. There's a good chance she'll move multiple times during her childhood whereas I stayed in the same school district throughout my education. Grandparent hugs are limited to summers and Christmas breaks; ballet recitals and birthday parties during the school year don't work well on Skype.

It's entirely possible that our daughters' lives would have been great had they been raised in a more traditional setting as my wife and I initially envisioned. However, raising them abroad has had benefits we could have never imagined when seeing those first pictures of Kaida five years ago. And while she now has the words, in English *and* Chinese, to ask so many questions to the world, there is not one language with the words to accurately answer them all. In the meantime, we smile back, knowing the journey is just beginning.

*Dave Wood, a native of Watertown, Wisconsin, teaches in Shanghai, China. He has taught high school social studies for 16 years, 6 years in the US and 10 years in South Korea and China.*

# OASIS
*Alli Poirot*

Drumbeats echoed off the red desert hills of Wadi Rum as we pumped our fists and jumped up and down to the sounds of Jaafar. The rock star, the nephew of King Abdullah II of Jordan, was filming his new music video "Oasis," and my friends and I were in it.

I had moved to Jordan to teach at a place *The New Yorker* called "Deerfield in the Desert"—a boarding school founded by the king and molded on the New England prep school model. Before the move, images of windswept desert, bedouin sheep-herders, and ancient Roman ruins filled my imagination. When I arrived, the wind was mostly blowing empty plastic trash bags that snagged on barbed wire fences watched by untended sheep. The landscape was dry and scraggly, the Roman ruins were kilometers away, and only grey concrete buildings lined the city. How would I find the poetic impressions of Jordan that I had imagined?

Through the wonders of the modern age, I had arrived ready with a handful of names of possible local friends—really, friends of friends back home. I had met Tala, an aspiring filmmaker, only once before when she unexpectedly called one day in October. Would I be interested in being an extra in a music video in Wadi Rum? Could I come tomorrow? And could I bring some friends?

Early the next morning, a few of my new colleagues and I, none of whom spoke any Arabic besides "shukran" and "marhaba," found an unmarked small bus on an unmarked small street near a generic traffic circle in Amman. I expected to be met by Tala with an explanation—in her perfect English—of what we were to do and how and where and when.

Instead, we knocked on the bus door, interrupting the sleeping driver's precious naptime. When we asked "Wadi Rum?," he gave us a curt nod, then brought his eyelids back to their resting position, arms still crossed over his chest. In spite of a lack of confidence that a video crew, or Tala for that matter, would be greeting us at the end of the journey, we still climbed inside the bus.

A few hours later, Wadi Rum greeted us with its full desert majesty. Tall twisted rocks gave way to endless oceans of sand. Reds and oranges bled into shadows of purple and blue. In the heart of this Martian landscape, we found the site of the music video: a refurbished train station paying homage to the role of the Arabs in the First World War. There was even a restored locomotive, a hulking iron relic that tourists could walk on and explore.

We foreign teachers bounced off the bus, excited for our roles as extras, but were patently ignored by the film staff and then finally told in Arabic to wait. It wasn't clear how long we would have to wait, just that they were shooting another section farther up the tracks. Unsure what to do, and without Tala to translate or to comfort us, we gamboled about on the restored train, took naps on desert rocks, and made sad puppy eyes at the film crew. An older man in a black leather jacket who worked at the tourist site asked about my age and marital status while my friends asked about lunch. After four hours of waiting, we finally got word that the shoot was about to begin.

Our role consisted of acting as fans of the king's nephew, arriving to an adoring crowd while singing on an open-air train car, made his grand appearance. The guitar riff was repeated again and again as the film crew took shots from different angles. We jumped up and down, screaming with adoration at Jaafar. We Americans were the most enthusiastic of the paltry crowd, yelling "I love you!" and turning our blissed-out faces to our hero as the train slid in to position. The crew noticed our acting skills and moved us front-and-center so the shots would capture our passionate fan activity.

During breaks we learned that the other "extras" were actually just crew and friends of crew. Tala never showed up, nor did most of Jordan, nor perhaps even most of the crew's friends. We were the only foreigners, but they loved our energy and idealism, our fists pumping and hips swaying through all twenty takes. They moved us from front-and-center to various other spots just to make it look like there were more people who were in the "Oasis." Though still operating on limited sleep and little food, it was sad when we found out there was not going to be a twenty-first take. We kissed the crew goodbye, waved to Jaafar, then boarded the bus back to Amman.

Months passed. The first semester became the second semester. The school year approached prom and graduation season.

Finally, in May, an email arrived from the video's director. I immediately ran into different faculty offices to show everyone. "Look! Our music video came out!" Because they had moved us around so much, our little crew of three got plenty of face time:

my pink jacket and my friend's right elbow were famous! "Oasis" started to be played on Top 40 local radio. Between Paramore and Sia was Jaafar, and we knew the song. Well, the one minute of it that we were in.

The song, though not especially profound or poetic ("I was nine in 1999, now I'm twenty-three, still dreaming about selling out the MSG, not talking about what they put on Chinese,") and the video, though quite contrived (the king's nephew standing on a train, singing to a small crowd in the middle of the desert), captures a moment in time, when Jordan wasn't what I expected yet occasionally was more than I could ever expect.

We snuck the song onto playlists at faculty dinners and parties, usually bringing a smile to our colleagues' faces any time they got "Jaafar-rolled." It became our Jordan anthem, getting plays morning, noon, or night, on weekdays and weekends. In fact, I suspect the three of us showing the video proudly and incessantly to our patient friends, family, and colleagues is the only reason it has 315 likes on YouTube today.

*Alli Poirot, a native of Massachusetts, teaches in Buenos Aires, Argentina. She has taught high school History, Social Studies, and Psychology for 15 years, 10 in the US and 5 in Jordan and Argentina.*

# THE LONG DISTANCE CALL
## *Tim Trotter*

My father methodically dials the numbers for the long distance call from Colorado to Korea. In 1977, this is a rather trying and uncertain process. The call goes through and someone answers. "Yobosayo?" The woman's voice manages to peek through the torrent of static on the line.

My father shouts, "This is David, Chong Hui's husband." It takes several seconds for the signal to navigate thousands of miles of cables before returning the effect of his announcement. "Ah!" Several excited voices can be heard in the background before my emo (aunt) Hyun Cha manages to climb on the phone and shout "Davy!" There are a lot of laughing voices in the background. He wonders if it is a birthday party. Even after 15 years of marriage to his Korean wife, my father can only manage a small amount of set phrases in Korean. My mother would laugh at the records he studied. "We don't talk that way!"

Next to my father, a Korean woman is nervously waiting. She is the wife of his colleague at the Air Force Base, and has graciously offered to help translate. After a few confusing exchanges, my father hands her the phone to deliver his message. She takes a moment to manage the weight of her payload, then starts in a friendly, deliberate voice, quickly explaining who she is. After the introductions are made and a brief, awkward pause transpires, she delivers the news. "Chong Hui has died from a catastrophic stroke."

The missile races to its destination. My father's eyes close, his breathing stops, his muscles tense as he braces himself. Then, inevitably, the shockwave of screams and confusion from Korea hit him.

I was 10 at the time. The two families would continue to ask for the aid of translators to write to each other, but each letter served as a reminder of a loss too painful for either side to bear. After a couple of years the letters stopped, and we lost contact altogether.

My brother and I grew up to be "Twinkies"—yellow on the outside and white on the inside. This always upset me, as I wanted to be truly of both cultures. When she was alive, I begged my mom to teach me Korean, but she refused. "You're American, so just learn English." America was embroiled in the Vietnam War, calling my father away for long stretches of time. My mother just wanted her two half-Korean boys to fit in.

Still, I was determined to learn, studying books and tapes whenever I could. After her death, this too came to an end, as every Korean I engaged would scoff at how poorly I spoke. To Koreans I was 100% American. To Americans I was Chinese.

Decades later, my wife and I landed jobs at an international school in Korea. The distance from home was worrisome, as were the threats from North Korea. However, for both of us, and our two young ¼-Korean children, this was a miraculous opportunity. Jen would teach literacy and I would be teaching mathematics in a society with a deep respect for the subject. The thought of being immersed in the culture I've longed to be more familiar with was nearly as exciting as the possibility of reconnecting with my lost family. My father, against his stoic nature, was wholly enthusiastic in his support.

The first year flew by. We were totally absorbed with the demands of a new school, new culture, and two young babies. This might even explain why I didn't seek out my lost family our second year either. Maybe. In the third year, it was obvious I was avoiding the search. I found it difficult to understand my feelings, but ultimately I was fearful. Fearful that my relatives would be disappointed that I could not speak Korean, that I didn't know any of the customs of my mother's culture, that they wouldn't accept me.

Once acknowledged, the fear of disappointment gave way to the fear of losing more time connecting with my family. I began the search. My father sent me all the information he had about my mother and her family, which amounted to not much: it was only her birth certificate, their marriage license, and a few letters. I accepted his apologies for how little he had to offer and began to work.

A reminder of the occupation before World War II, her birth certificate is in Japanese, a language few Koreans can read these days. The marriage license proved equally useless. The best clue we had was the address of my *emo* in Suwon, a mere 30 minutes from where we now lived. Vivid memories of that house are imprinted in my mind from summers we spent there when I was a young child. Suwon was so close that we decided to drive there and see if we could find the house ourselves. No such luck. The house and the whole street were bulldozed many years earlier to make way for new apartments.

Finally, I turned to the business office at our school for help. It should have been the first thing I tried, but they were always so very busy. At the end of a staff meeting, the Korean director threw out that I was searching for my lost relatives should any of them want to take on the extra duty.

Unexpectedly, a woman immediately volunteered. "Karen," her English name, was the assistant to the middle school principal. Like so many of her peers, Karen was highly overqualified for her position, and welcomed my challenge.

We met and I gave her the thin folder of information I possessed. After scanning the documents, she kindly, politely, stated what I already knew: this was going to be a long shot. Still, she was full of confidence and left me with a faint feeling of hope.

A few days later, Karen asked to meet. She came to my classroom and when we sat down, her face turned serious. She explained that she searched some governmental and public databases and came up with nothing. The most complete database, she explained, belonged to the police, and is strictly off limits to anyone but the police. My face fell. The reality that this might not ever happen grabbed ahold of me. But, with my eyes glued to the floor, Karen spoke again.

"My father is the Chief of Police," she said, "and as a favor to me he found some addresses."

I was stunned. Seeing my reaction, Karen gave a warm smile, probably the only thing on Earth that could melt the iron-clad heart of a city police chief. "There are numerous men with your uncle's name living in Suwon, but seven addresses were chosen as the most likely."

To each we sent a letter explaining who I was and why I was searching for my mother's family. All seven letters were accompanied with an old photo of my mother and Karen's cell number. The only thing left was to wait. On the outside I tried to appear patient and calm. On the inside I was a wreck. All the long years of not knowing, all the questions, the longing, all reached a heart-pounding crescendo. I wasn't sure I could handle it if it failed.

I tried to distract myself with work. A week passed when I got a call on the phone in my classroom. It was Karen. She wanted me to see her as soon as I was able. I left to meet her immediately, leaving the ungraded papers scattered about my desk. I found her outside of the office listening on her cell phone. When she saw me, Karen covered the phone microphone with her hand and told me the news—my *emo* was on the phone!

She handed the phone to me.

"Emo?" I asked.

A slight pause.

Then an explosion of emotion.

Hyun Cha spoke so fast, so passionately, that she didn't take a breath for what must have been several minutes. My Korean was still very limited. I couldn't follow the words, but I imagine they were full of all the hopes, worries, and regrets she'd carried these many years. With every fiber of my being I wanted to respond in kind, but didn't have the words to do so. I told her I loved her and missed her in English, managed a "goodbye" in Korean, and passed the phone back to Karen.

A couple of weeks later my father receives a long distance call from Korea. On the line he hears what must be a party. It's a family reunion. I'm there, along with my mother's two surviving sisters, and seven of my nine cousins. The youngest cousin is able to translate for everyone, though most are happy just giving huge grins and long, strong hugs. They are all enamored with my two kids, as well as Jen's ability to eat kimchi. I help relay all the stories everyone can remember back and forth across the phone. We recall how my brother and I used to play hide-and-seek with my cousins in my emo's house for hours on end, how we used to catch frogs while the women washed the family clothes in the Suwon River, how they loved—and fought—over the care packages my mom would send from the States full of the latest fashions, books, flashlights, mini radios, and games. There is no awkwardness, no divide. Only joy and a deep sense of family. It is clear we will never let time and space divide us again, and that we will make it a priority to make up for lost time. The phone finally makes its way to everyone at the reunion. Everyone finishes sending their love. My father hangs up, and the dark clouds of the past lighten and fade.

*Tim Trotter, a Denver, Colorado native, teaches mathematics in Istanbul, Turkey. He has taught high school mathematics for 20 years, 5 in the US and 15 in Mexico, Costa Rica, South Korea and Turkey.*

# STORIES FROM MY NAME
*Matthew James Friday*

I was panicking and trying to hide it.

I was on the front row of a packed auditorium, sharing the row with other, more experienced, professional storytellers. We were all in a university in northern Thailand as part of an international storytelling festival, and in a few minutes I needed to stand up and tell a story to a room of politely excited student teachers, their tutors, and friends...none of whom spoke English. So my story would need to be translated on the spot by Jumliet, the co-director of the festival whom I had just met. She had a purring smile and a cheeky glint in her eye, a Thai Cheshire Cat. I had never told a story with a translator before.

In addition, none of the audience were children. I am a storyteller for elementary-age children, and, at that point, I was a grade 3 teacher in an international school in China. My particular style of storytelling involves the children as participants, acting out the story as I tell it, which they love. Well, on this warm February day there were no children, no volunteers, and no way I could back out. My loyal wife Jill—also an international school teacher—sat several rows back, whispering her love for me, love found when we had met each other at an international school in Bonn, Germany several years before.

The show was about to start with Margaret MacDonald, one of the most experienced and well-known storytellers on the circuit. It was a unique chance to learn from the master, except I was sitting there panicking, running through my mind my "set list" of folktales and fables, begging for some kind of revelation to instruct me about which one would be best suited to this audience. I was clueless. So instead I just listened to Margaret open the festival. I let her words roll over me. I tuned into something she was saying about how we are all storytellers (true) and how we all have stories to tell (very true) and how we can all start by telling our own story.

I felt slapped by that statement. *Tell your own story.* As soon as I repeated those words, the answer bubbled up: the story of my family name, Friday. Why am I called Mr. Friday? The question I am asked in every school I visit, by every class I teach, by every student I meet, over and over again.

Just as I was firming up this radical departure from my rehearsed storytelling plan, a familiar shiver of doubt and self-disgust washed over me. I hate my name. I hate the attention it causes. I hate the sniggers that I hear when it's first announced. Could I overcome this and talk about it in front of several hundred strangers, via a translator? I had a few minutes to decide.

I have hated my name ever since grade 2 (year 3) in England when my teacher, Mr. R., gave permission to my classmates to mock me ceaselessly after he did the same. He was a small man with a pointed beard like Ming the Merciless, only Mini-Ming. The other children had often mocked "Friday" but it had grown stale as a source of fun—until Mr. R. added his own stunted brand of witticism to the cause. He also complicated the mockery by calling me "Matilda Friday," Matilda being the name of the type of tanks my grandfather had driven across Africa in the Second World War.

Two things had ended this punishment. Firstly, I stood up for myself and made fun of his name. It was hardly a stunning riposte worthy of Flash Gordon, but it had caused him to cease long enough for the second act. My parents complained to the headteacher, who had then ordered him to desist.

My name was called. Polite applause rippled through the auditorium. No laughter. Unusual. A good start. I stood up, slightly giddy with adrenaline and hope. Taking Margaret's advice was one of the best decisions I ever made as a storyteller.

I began to tell how we had learned the story of our family name from my father's years of amateur sleuthing through local government birth records as he reconstructed our working class family tree back to mid-Victorian times. My Victorian ancestor was, as far as we can tell, an orphan raised in an orphanage in London or southeastern England, given the name Friday, perhaps for a religious reason but more likely due to the fact he had been delivered on a Friday (children often think I was born on a Friday or I love Fridays). This fact prompted the obvious question: how come there are no families of Sundays? Tuesdays? Wednesdays? I have met *Mundays* in England, but never Mondays. So why just Fridays? And the fact that there are random groups of unrelated Fridays around the country supports the theory of a possible Victorian naming pattern.

At this point, the storyteller's embellishment privilege kicked in. I created pictures for my audience of Victorian orphanages, the cramped classrooms and intimidating canteens, the kindly but stern-looking nurses. The yarn continued with little George (or was it Edward?) Friday being bullied in the orphanage for his name, so the manager decided not to use days of the week again. But older Georgie or Eddie showed a skill for teaching younger orphans, a skill I have carried forward. And there ended the story, more or less.

My retelling of our family myth received warm applause, smiles, nodding. People seemed to be connecting to it in a manner I was surprised by. It buoyed me with confidence and I launched into the fable of "How the Lion Got his Roar" with the help of Jumliet, who seemed to have the uncanny ability to translate *before* I said the line, which the audience found hilarious. A new double act was formed, and it lasted the whole festival, from university lecture rooms to community gatherings on golden beaches. I learned how much fun having a translator can be.

But this is not the only surprise I was in for.

After the festival opening show, an excellent storyteller from Burma—Thantzin Soe—told me that part of his name also translated as Mr. Friday. In Burma one's birthday is incorporated into one's name, so Mr. Friday is not something people mock or really remark upon. This Mr. Friday was proud of his name and grateful for my story and wanted to reassure me that Friday is a gift, not a curse. Carry that gift proudly, tell the story, own the name. Be Mr. Friday. Use your name and let it evoke surprise, laughter, respect. Here was the other truth my international teaching friends and wife had been telling me for some years, but I had not been able to hear: *Mr. Friday is a cool name for a teacher.*

So I returned to Guangzhou and took back ownership of my name. Many Chinese children in international schools adopt Western names. I adopted the Chinese translation of Friday— Xingqiwu (singcheewoo).

The Friday connections continued. Six months later, after our marriage, Jill and I took a honeymoon trekking holiday in the

Himalayas. Our patient and effortlessly impressive Sherpa guide was called Dawa, or "Monday," and his son was Pemba— Saturday. He loved the fact I was called Friday! No issue for the Sherpa people.

When we left our school in China, our generous Chinese teaching assistant friend Jojo commissioned a local calligrapher to paint my name in Chinese characters. It sits above our bed, a reminder for me to be proud of my name and the many people it connects me with as I continue this incredible international teaching journey.

Mr. Friday: finally, a name I don't hate or shrink from. A name I am proud of.

*Matthew James Friday, a native of England, teaches Grade 5 in an international school in Lugano, Switzerland. He has taught in all elementary school grades for 11 years: 5 in London, UK; 4 in Germany and 2 in China. He is also a published poet and professional storyteller for children, and has visited many schools in countries all over the world.*

# DON'T DAR LA PAPAYA
*Danielle Allie*

The doctor picked up my right hand and frowned.

"Your skin looks a bit orange."
"Huh. Interesting."

She placed my hand next to hers. "See? Look at your skin tone compared to mine. Orange." She was right. I was turning orange.

In the first week of teacher orientation in Medellín, Colombia, new hires were warned to never "dar la papaya." This meant that we should be careful with our things, as placing a cell phone on a table or carrying a wallet in a back pocket would be to tempt a thief—to "give them the papaya." I attempted to heed the advice of locals as best I could, but it didn't take long for me to realize how difficult it would be to avoid the actual fruit.

Before living in Colombia, I had never tried papaya. I'm not even sure I could have identified the large orange fruit at Whole Foods. I grew up in Wisconsin with cheese, brats, and beer. In my family, fresh fruit and vegetables were something that had been out of the can for less than an hour. But when I moved overseas, first to Honduras and then to Colombia, my diet slowly evolved.

My addiction to the fruit was slow to take hold. Early on, a trip to the grocery store might end with half of a papaya at the bottom of the cart. I would carefully scoop out the tiny green seeds (thanks, YouTube) and slice the fruit into strips before cubing it and placing it neatly in Tupperware. It made for the perfect hot-weather treat.

A quarter of a papaya made for a sensible snack, but there are seven days in a week and at least five days between trips to the grocery store. As I settled into life in the "eternal spring," a place where the temperature rarely requires a jacket or even a sweater, my cravings for something cold and sweet intensified. A half of a papaya, even one large one, stopped sufficing. I needed to buy more papaya.

About two years into living in Colombia, a group of friends planned a trip to the Amazon. The rainforest is home to at least 3,000 fruits, dozens of which were beautifully presented to us on the kitchen table of a family from Puerto Nariño. None of them was papaya. A week of sampling at least twenty exotic, tasty fruits that I could never possibly remember the name of, and I was still craving just one thing: papaya.

Once a week, my friend and I would meet and walk to a farmer's market and carry the produce home in backpacks. But forget about carrying the papayas. They required a special trip to the grocery store near my apartment. As my thirst for papaya grew, so did my shopping list and so did the amount of time I spent getting those groceries.

Unloading and finding room for the large fruit in the fridge soon became a twenty-minute project. No longer was I pulling out the cutting board, and forget about the Tupperware. I attacked each one with a spoon, scooping it out in chunks and gobbling it up as I leaned against the counter in the kitchen.

I also started to consume papaya in bed because it was more than a hot-weather treat. It was an all-the-time addiction. My husband was less than pleased.

"Dani, did you throw-up last night?"
"No, why?" I knew why.
"It smells like vomit in here. What is that?"
"I don't know." I knew.
"Is that a papaya skin on your bedside table?"
"It might be." It was.
"They offer divorces online for like $100 now, you know."

Months later, as I sat before my dermatologist with skin the hue of an Oompa Loompa, I had been caught.

I let the doctor run through her list of usual orange-skin suspects—self-tanner, oranges, carrots, sweet potatoes—before I broke.

"You eat *how many* papayas in a week?"

After being advised to consume a variety of fruit, or to just cut back on papaya in general, I got the hint. I'd have to change my ways. This, of course, was easier said than done.

The only cure for my addiction, it turned out, was a move to China, where the fruit is wrapped in far too much plastic and doesn't taste like its Colombia-fresh friends.

Whether I perfectly adhered to the "dar la papaya" rule or I was just plain lucky, I experienced nothing but safety in that beautiful country I called home for years. I made lifelong friends, grew to cherish the mountains, and learned to speak a second language. My skin may have changed colors, but my cell phone never disappeared off a table.

And as for the food in my new home, China—the dumplings, the lotus root, the noodles—I can only hope, with fingers crossed, that they don't start to taste *too* good.

*Danielle Allie, a native of Sturgeon Bay, Wisconsin, currently teaches in Shanghai, China. She has been an elementary homeroom teacher and middle school humanities teacher for the past eleven years in Honduras, Colombia, and China.*

# A SMALL THING
*Ken Turner*

It is a quiet thing, a modest thing, fragile and flat and small enough to fit in a drawer. And it is without color, unlike the other objects in the room: Afghan carpets glowing with rose and madder, deep indigo, and rich rusty ochre.

The storefront itself is nondescript, just one in a row of cement-block shops, two doors down from another, better-known carpet shop and around the corner from a small Chinese restaurant. It is the 1990s. Islamabad, Pakistan's relatively new, still raw capital, a city laid out in grids and sectors with impersonal alphabetic designations (G-3, F-8), is full of these concrete strips assembled into "markets." This is Jinnah Market, named for the country's revered founder. Since the Soviet withdrawal and subsequent civil war in Pakistan's neighbor, this country and city have been hosting increasing numbers of refugees, some of them managing to survive by selling tribal carpets salvaged or smuggled from their homeland.

As I approach the door I realize I'm not sure what first drew me into this particular shop: perhaps a small, unusually colored Bokhara hanging in the single window? By now, though, I am acquainted with this space, and as I open the door and enter, I feel the familiarity. The old wall-mounted air conditioning unit stuttering and wheezing, condensation slowly dripping into a green plastic bowl; the unmistakable carpet-shop smell, close, musty, with an animal undertone of slightly damp wool; the boxy piles of layered rugs in the corners of the room. And to the left of the door, facing the room, the cheap wooden desk from which Ahmed is already rising, his hand extended in greeting.

"Asalaam Alaikum, my friend. How are you today?"

"Wa'alaikum es-salaam, my friend. I am fine, and you?"

"Very fine. Come, sit, have some tea. What can I show you this afternoon?"

Ahmed is tall and broad-shouldered, wearing as he always does a plain white shalwar kameez, the long loose tunic and baggy pants that are the national dress of Pakistan and Afghanistan. He is barefoot. His hair is brown and his eyes are as green as mine, not uncommon features for a Pathan from eastern Afghanistan. He stoops to begin the familiar routine, placing the small, battered metal teapot on the electric plate on the floor by his desk. Soon he is handing me a tiny china cup of sweet cardamom tea, the first of many we are likely to consume this afternoon. The first part of the Ritual Of Tea And Conversation Over Carpets has begun.

"Do you have anything new? Or something I haven't seen that you think I might like?"

Holding my tea, I sit on a small wooden chair. Ahmed crosses the room to the piles of rugs and rummages through. He picks one, turns, and with a flourish, unfurls it in the air like some glorious heavy flag, extending it across the floor at my feet. The second part of the Ritual, Conversation Over Carpets, is about to commence.

Nice. I haven't seen a pattern like this before. That bright blue of the ground is unusual, and the design of splashy red and white flowers connected by yellow vines looks like a trellis.

"Tell me about this carpet."

"The pattern is Mina Khani, Persian, from western Afghanistan, near Herat. Old one, very fine colors."

As we continue to discuss the rug, I reflect on all I have learned from Ahmed. About the roots of this remarkable folk art: nomadic life in the harsh landscapes of Central Asia and the need for soft, warm, portable surfaces for sitting, eating, and sleeping. About the traditional patterns, especially the intricate octagonal forms called guls, originally derived from flowers but now often referred to as "elephants' feet." About natural and synthetic dyes and how to tell the difference, about fringes and selvages, about repairs. I notice this carpet has been repaired, with careful stitching of two small rips near one edge. This evidence of long use, of human attention to a cherished and useful object, makes the rug all the more compelling to me.

"And what about that old prayer rug I looked at last time? Could I see it again?"

"Of course, my friend."

As Ahmed settles it on the floor, I see again why I was drawn to this rug. Very dark at first glance, in the light it begins to reveal its hidden beauty: the deep blue ground glows, setting off notched rosettes of dark crimson and a light tawny brown. An inner rectangle delicately outlined in white takes up three-quarters of the surface, and from this projects another, smaller rectangle. This section represents the mihrab of a mosque, oriented in the direction of Mecca before prayer. The pile is slightly worn in three places, where the two hands and forehead have repeatedly pressed as the worshipper prostrated himself. The selvage curves in toward one end where the weaver inadvertently narrowed the width; one horizontal band is woven in light orange, showing where she ran out of red yarn and substituted what she had at hand. Deeply personal, this handmade piece of art bears strong witness to its maker as well as its user. I am falling in love, although it will take one more visit to confirm that feeling and begin the long, friendly process of arriving at a fair price.

But of course I visit this shop for more than just these carpets. I come for Ahmed, too, for the pleasure of his company, for what I'm learning from him about the people I'm living among, for our quiet, tentative, slowly developing friendship. We are very different, he and I. Very different. Some of his deeply held values are easy for me to understand, to respect and admire: hospitality, trust, devotion to family. His shop, for example, is a family business, its inventory collected over time. The carpets around me are the accumulated assets—the stocks, bonds, IRAs, so to speak—of a large clan, entrusted for the moment to Ahmed. Yet he will happily encourage me to take home carpets worth thousands of dollars to live with and consider for purchase—without specifying any time limit or asking for any sort of collateral, or for that matter, even my address.

Other aspects of his life I approach with more ambivalence and hesitation. He knows I have a wife and two daughters; I know he has a wife and young son. He knows my wife works at the international school with me, where my daughters study, and that we live far from the rest of our family, visiting only in the summer. I know his wife and child live with other family members in one of the sprawling refugee townships past Peshawar, near the Afghan border; he visits them when he can. I know little else about his family. His culture, after all, is one with rigid gender divisions and expectations, ones I find baffling and, to be honest, offensive. Women make carpets, men sell them; women must be isolated and protected by their male relatives; virtuous women should remain shielded from the view of outsiders, especially men. Even here in relatively cosmopolitan Islamabad I occasionally see burka-clad women in the street, and each time it is still a shock.

Our carpet discussions are finished for now, although I know I'll be back to look at that prayer rug. My teacup is empty. I make a motion to rise.

"Just a minute, my friend. I want to show you something before you leave."

Ahmed crosses to the desk, opens a drawer, and pulls out a small rectangle of paper. He approaches me and places the photo in my hand. It is a black-and-white snapshot of a young woman in an embroidered shalwar kameez with a dupatta shawl draped across her neck. Her lustrous black hair is uncovered. She looks directly into the camera, confident and composed, with just the barest hint of a smile.

"My friend, this is my wife."

It is just a small thing, a quiet thing, a simple thing really, one man showing another a picture of his wife. But as a stranger and a guest in this part of the world, as a non-Muslim in an intensely Muslim culture, as a casual American among these proud, private, somewhat formal people, I find this modest gesture disarming. This small thing makes my heart swell, if even just a little.

*After teaching high school social studies and English for nearly four decades around the world, Ken Turner has come full circle. Born in central Florida, he taught for 13 years in the US and 24 in Congo (Zaire), Pakistan, Ivory Coast, Venezuela, China, and the Dominican Republic. He is now back in central Florida, happily retired.*

# COFFEE: A CARACAS LOVE STORY
*Maureen McCann*

I fell in love with coffee, Spanish, and my husband in Venezuela.

First came the coffee.

When I lived in Venezuela in the 1990s, there was a bakery named Alicantina a few blocks from the international school where I taught. Inside Alicantina I learned to order a small *café con leche* (coffee with milk), standing elbow-to-elbow with Venezuelans on a Saturday morning. Here is where I first chatted in Spanish and adjusted my ear to the Caraqueño accent, *s*'s dropping left and right, double entendres exploding in peals of laughter.

Alicantina lacked seating...on purpose. The coffee bar was polished wood, perfect for leaning loners. A customer first paid at the cash register, then found a space at the crowded bar to order a coffee and pastry from one of the many uniformed ladies who worked the counter. An enormous mirror hung across the back of the bar, providing coffee drinkers a view of the action behind them. One tiny woman stood on a stool and worked the espresso machine, banging the metal cup of frothy milk, making it hiss its foreign coffee culture importance, exotic to me, a newly-arrived *gringa* teacher from North Carolina.

In Venezuela, a person may stop by a bakery and order an espresso-sized coffee in any gorgeous shade of brown the drinker prefers. Specifying the shade of brownness is key. A *negrito* or espresso is pure coffee, no milk. A *marrón* is dark khaki with a bit of milk. Meanwhile, a *con leche* is golden, a balance of coffee and milk. In the same way, Venezuelans may refer to each other using these same expressions as terms of endearment. A darker-skinned Venezuelan may be called *negrito,* and a woman with a beach tan may be described as one who has a *café con leche* complexion. The culture is even referred to as a *café con leche* one, a society where the mixture of races has made the population beautiful. Love of coffee equalizes, and coffee drinkers with all manner of skin tones are welcome to down a cup. They might stand up or lean against a bakery counter for a chat, then dash out the door in under ten minutes, only a little late for the next destination—and any Venezuelan understands that stopping for a coffee is reason enough to be a little late.

Then came the Spanish.

After the love affair with coffee began, love of the Spanish language, spoken or sung with a Venezuelan accent, soon followed. The quick rolling *r*'s and the passion of the language invaded my heart and settled there permanently. Venezuelans speak not only with their voices but with their hands and bodies, too. An exasperated statement of the obvious may be punctuated with hands over the belly, raised eyebrows, and a pause. A female hand fluttering out of the car window gives the driver permission to proceed up a one-way street with no complaints. They are a boisterous bunch of extroverts, and I wanted desperately to understand and participate in their conversations. It took me several months to garner the courage to actually speak the Spanish I had learned in school to a real Venezuelan. Thankfully, they were never snobbish when I attempted to speak their type of Spanish, known as *Castellano*. If I admitted to feeling embarrassed by describing some ridiculous event that befell me and mistakenly used the adjective *embarazada*, meaning "pregnant," a Venezuelan would make light of it and correct me, using the correct word *verguenza*. But they would not interrupt the flow of my story. Miraculously, Venezuelans understood me. My understanding their machine-gun-fast Spanish was the challenge.

I didn't intend to fall in love with coffee or Venezuelan-style Spanish, but I did, right there in that bakery where every other Venezuelan seemed to know someone. Standing there at the Alicantina counter, I began to entertain the possibility that I could happily teach there forever, living in my apartment near the school with its windows open to street noises and the feathered cacophony of birds arguing in nearby flowering branches.

And last, came the husband.

When I first met my future husband at a friend's wedding, I saw espresso-colored eyes in a porcelain cup, steamy and profound. He was of Spanish and Dutch heritage, tall and fair-skinned with the dark hair and serious eyes of a Spaniard. A longtime friend of the groom, he asked me to dance merengue at the reception held on a full moon night on the Venezuelan island of Margarita. "Dancing merengue" is quite an exaggeration; actually, he politely danced around me and made it look like I danced merengue.

This man surprised me. He liked my American punctuality and even my freckles. Ironically, in a land where lateness is an art form, he was always on time. He spoke English fairly well. At first, there was even a subtle relationship-language arm wrestle in which we were quietly participating. Alas, English won, even though we also speak Spanish at home.

One of our first dates was for breakfast on a Saturday before he left the city for his family farm. I had never been asked out on a morning date. I stood beside him at the counter in this country that now felt like home and proudly introduced him to Alicantina. After I ordered my *café con leche pequeño*, I listened carefully to learn which coffee he preferred. He ordered orange juice. In a stunning irony, the man who would become my husband was the first Venezuelan I had ever met who did not like coffee!

*Maureen McCann, a native of Raleigh, North Carolina, teaches in Hong Kong. She has been a librarian for thirteen years and has also taught middle school language arts and social studies. She has been happily teaching in the "middle" for thirty years, 5 in the US, and 25 in Costa Rica, Venezuela, and Hong Kong.*

# STATISTICALLY UNLIKELY
*Danielle Bedard*

"Statistically, it's unlikely that any of the tragedies you're imagining would actually happen. From now on, when you're feeling anxious, it might help to remind yourself of that."

The panic attacks had started about three months prior to that conversation with my therapist. And I had to admit, she had a point. Thinking about the scenarios that had triggered my attacks in the past, it was highly unlikely that I would be trampled by a crowd in an underground train station in Hong Kong; thousands of flights took off and landed safely every day; and scuba divers did not generally succumb to the bends while diving at ten meters in Bali.

Over the next weeks, I would silently repeat my therapist's reminder and successfully slow my heart rate, dry my palms, and circumvent the full-body terror. Every time, I felt the pride of having won a battle.

But my greatest test would take place about two months later during a dive trip in Thailand, just off the coast of Koh Tao Island. My dive buddy Jordan and I were all smiles as we boarded the boat. Jordan's was genuine; he was eager to get another dive under his belt, and diving in Thailand had always been a dream of his. My smile was tentative at best. Although I had found great success in maintaining my calm on land, this was going to be my first diving experience in over six months.

As I sat on the boat, taking deep breaths and thinking reassuring thoughts, our dive master lumbered over to introduce himself. While he exchanged pleasantries with Jordan, I had a chance to size him up—an eager handshake, genuine smile, and rosy cheeks. I tried to ignore his bloodshot eyes and what seemed to be pieces of seaweed hidden amongst his few remaining wisps of hair. My glance moved down to his torso and his bulging stomach, which was just barely contained by a too tight, too short Smurfs t-shirt. His baggie shorts hadn't been laundered recently, possibly ever. He wore no shoes.

I felt my chest tighten.

The man looked about fifty, but with his apparent lifestyle, he could easily have been a twenty-five-year-old who had whittled away at his health with reckless abandon. I was certain there were heart attack statistics to support my new theory that he would suffer from a cardial infarction any day now, likely on this dive. *Nope. Don't go there. Deep breath in, one, two, three, four. Deep breath out, one, two, three, four.* Grungy and overweight dive masters successfully lead dives every day.

"I'm sorry. I missed your name," I said as soon as I had regained my focus.

"It's Chang! Nice to meet you!" he said, thrusting a chubby hand in my direction.

85

"Did you say Chang? As in the Thai beer, Chang?"

"That's the one! My namesake!"

I stopped myself from asking how exactly a person earns the nickname of a cheap local beer.

Before I had time to recover, Chang bent over to pull on his wetsuit. As he did, something yellow caught my eye, right above his pale, slightly exposed posterior. Without thinking, I leaned in slightly to confirm that I was in fact looking at a Bart Simpson tattoo. A Bart Simpson tramp stamp.

*Deep breath in, one, two, three, four. Deep breath out, one, two, three, four.*

As Chang reached down for his right fin, he exclaimed, "Oh wow! Where did that come from?" He was chuckling and aiming his chin at his right foot. "I guess I got another tattoo last night. That looks great!"

In agitated awe, I moved my gaze from Chang's backside to the top of his foot. A large Pac-Man stared back at me.

Chang chattered on, "What a night last night. It's all a bit of a blur. When I woke up on the beach an hour ago, I had no idea where I was!"

*Deep breath in, one, two, three, four. Deep breath out, one, two, three, four.*

What kind of statistics are there on poor decision-making? As in, if a grown man puts no stock in hygiene, inks his body with cartoon characters in a blackout state, and drinks enough beer to be named after it, what is the likelihood that he will make solid decisions underwater?

I looked over at Jordan, expecting to see a glimpse of the terror that I was feeling, but all I saw was detached amusement in his expression. Clearly, I was overthinking this.

We suited up, performed our safety checks, and dropped into the water, slowly descending to the bottom.

*Deep breath in, one, two, three, four. Deep breath out, one, two, three, four.*

This was going to be fine. The visibility was excellent, there was no current, and we were surrounded by a kaleidoscope of small, non-threatening sea creatures. I began to relax as I followed Chang through the water.

A shiny object on the ocean floor caught my eye. Swimming with more bravery than I felt, two quick kicks brought me closer, and I reached out to pick it up. A dive knife! What a find! I swam up to Chang, pulling on one of his fins to get his attention.

Chang was just as excited when he realised what I had found. Then his look of enthusiasm suddenly changed to recognition. He patted quickly around his waist at his own tool belt, finding his knife sheath empty. Recognition was replaced with gratitude when he took his knife from my hand and placed it back where it belonged.

My pulse quickened, the first sign of panic. Rapidly sucking in puffs of air from my regulator, I reviewed the possible scenarios where Chang's incompetence and/or apparent health issues could lead to my own death. Statistically speaking, things were not looking good.

As my anxiety took grip, the lengths of my inhales began to outlast my exhales. With my balloon-like lungs full to bursting, I rose toward the surface. Very quickly, instead of swimming in line with Jordan and Chang, I was floating above them.

When Chang noticed, he approached me with the extra weight that dive masters commonly carry with them. This would fix the problem. With my hands shaking in fear, I opened the pocket on my vest and placed the weight inside. I let go of it, only to see the weight fall through the water and disappear into the depths below.

Chang was surprised, but not concerned. He leaned forward, gave a barely noticeable shrug of his shoulders, and handed me another weight from his vest. Feeling confident that I was unlikely to make the same mistake twice, with a few kicks, he dove below me to where Jordan waited.

Again, I opened the pocket on my vest with one hand. Grasping the weight with the other hand, I eased it into the pocket. I did not notice the hole in the fabric. When I let go, I couldn't believe it when the weight began to fall through the water in the general direction of Chang.

The square weight fell more like a leaf than a three-pound piece of lead. It glided slowly in one direction and then another. At times, it would pick up speed when it became perfectly vertical, but then it would flip to horizontal and continue its coasting path.

I felt a wave of calm flow through me as I was reminded of summer days watching "The Price is Right" and my favorite game, Plinko, where a chip is dropped from the top of a large pegged board. The goal is to get the chip to pass down to the bottom into the slots below labelled with various amounts of money. The contestants on the show would anxiously wring their hands, watching the chip dip to the left, then the right, and then straight down into a slot. I would giddily watch from the safety of my couch, laughing at their naivete. From my vast experience watching this game, I knew that, statistically, that chip had almost no chance of hitting its target.

Curiously, just as I finished that thought, the weight took a dive to the left and bounced off Chang's balding head.

*No. It can't be.*

Chang looked up, confused by the unexpected blow. But with a quick brush of a hand over his head, he confirmed he was unharmed and enthusiastically gave the dive sign for "I'm okay." Surprisingly, the accidental missile had done less harm than his binge-drinking marathon the night before.

Having faced near-tragedy without injury, the three of us decided to end the dive for the day.

My therapist's advice had worked. The distraction of thinking about statistical probabilities had gotten me through twenty-seven minutes at ten meters of depth. An increased heart rate, a few extra breaths. But no panic attack. I survived the dive with Chang. Statistically, that should not have happened.

*Danielle Bedard, a native of Sandwich, Massachusetts has been teaching elementary school for 15 years; 3 in the U.S., and 12 in South Korea, Tunisia, and Hong Kong.*

# MR. FIX-IT'S GRANDMOTHER, MY THANKS TO YOU
*Kimberly Russell*

One afternoon in the first few weeks at our new school in São Paulo, I heard the rhythmic tapping of Tetris coming from the living room. Eli, my normally confident, puckish son, was slouched and mindlessly striking keys on his laptop. "Why are you home so early from workout club?" I asked. Without raising his impish hazel eyes or missing a beat in his game, he responded flatly, "I don't have a partner."

"Can't you take turns with someone else's partner?" I suggested.

"They have their own partners, routines, and systems. It's okay."

"Well, the next time, perhaps you could bring another classmate with you?" He looked up with eyes as dull and lifeless as the polluted Pinheiros River, only long enough to explain, "Everyone I care to know is already there."

Initially they had been on board with our decision to go abroad again, but I should have known that by the time the contracts were signed, documents notarized, and boxes packed, they would have changed their minds. As the departure date neared, my teenage sons began to voice their fervent appreciation of life in America and their Quaker Friends school. They claimed they had connections from their elementary school days and even added that the quiet meeting times at their school were good for them! But these reactions paled in comparison to their initial reactions upon learning our new destination. I can still hear my husband announcing "It's Brazil!" to the boys minutes after our final, exciting Skype interview.

Eli responded with an exasperated, "This is final? No input from us?" Noah added, "I thought you were considering someplace interesting like Vietnam." To be fair, they had already lived in Peru for two years of elementary school. Moreover, I suppose after attending school for the past four years in India, any place on Earth might seem less exotic.

After a lonely first semester in South America, we all returned to the States for Christmas break and stayed at an Airbnb. One night I was forced to call the owner, Michael, to fix the support bar on the sunken IKEA sofa. He arrived enthusiastically, his wide athletic shoulders and smile of equal measure filling the doorway with energy. As he was diagnosing the needed repair, I made small talk with this entrepreneurial Mr. Fix-it. "You have kids?"

Michael's expression stayed surprisingly happy as he explained, "My son moved to California to start a business, but it isn't going well, so understandably he is depressed." I nodded knowingly and repeated the condolence, "You're only ever as happy as your unhappiest child."

I had read these words years before; the phrase resonated and stuck with me and I believed it wholeheartedly. When my kids hit a low, I fell with them. When they were not thriving, I shriveled and thought I wasn't allowed to thrive either. I figured Michael would nod and agree with my wise child-rearing maxim. Instead, he looked at me with a broadening smile and responded, "Ah, no. Show them joy."

I was taken aback. I sat back solidly in my chair in order to absorb what he was saying. I hadn't thought of that. I thought sympathetic misery was the only course. The "Oy vey iz mir!" was the only way. "How do you do that, exactly?"

Michael excused himself to run out in the chilly December air to the hardware store across the street. I waited for his return, unmoving in thought, still glued to the chair. He entered the door, still with laughing eyes. He seemed to delight in once again lowering his body to the floor to solve the mystery of the broken couch, so I leaned in and asked, "What is the secret to you being so happy while your son is struggling and you are stuck fixing a sofa on a cold winter night?"

With a smile-creased face and serene expression he explained, "My Haitian grandmother taught us all to always look at the bright side of everything and be joyful. It is the secret to our success." Inspired by the words, I sat in silence as Michael joyfully tinkered and finally succeeded in repairing the sofa.

The sofa was fixed, but not everything else was. Back in Brazil, I continued to walk around with a heart that felt heavier than a dead donkey. Night after night, I felt responsible for the two rainclouds parked in my living room. Finally, one night I decided to relieve the weight of my burden with a candid talk.

"Guys," I began. "I acknowledge that moving you for the last two years of high school without your full, enthusiastic agreement on the location may not have been the best decision, but it was made with all of us in mind."

Two sets of sidelong glances and a puh-lease no-more-Bloom-Where-You-Are-Planted-lecture stare were all I got. The thick silence that followed told me how angry they still were. Finally, Eli piped up with, "We understand that this is a good opportunity, but we still would rather be in the States." Channeling Michael's approach to life, I responded, "Well, I am going to be joyful here, and I hope you can be, too."

I took tennis, yoga and ballet lessons—all in Portuguese—and through these experiences, I took joy in getting to know Brazilians, among the gentlest and kindest people I have met. I took joy in teaching and learning from both the local and international kids at my school. Dragging my sons along when I could entice them, I found joy in São Paulo by attending art exhibits and even a photography exhibit where my girlhood crush Julian Lennon kissed my cheek. I stayed out all night at a drag show that started at 3 a.m.; I saw Sting perform, accompanied by some of his friends from the rainforest; I was an enthusiastic spectator at the Sambódromo during Carnaval.

In our second year, during another Christmas break in the States, my oldest accompanied me to a running shoe store. I asked him, "Noah, remember when we jogged together most every morning in India?" He offered an indirect glance to acknowledge my question. "Remember how it woke you up enough to eat breakfast and you felt better?" He shrugged a *sort of.* "What if you got a pair of shoes and joined the very first track team at your school? You know running is good for your mood and health, and it could connect you with some other people." Noah compliantly pointed to a couple of pairs of shoes to try on. He slipped on a pair of powder blue New Balance trainers and dutifully but unenthusiastically trotted around the small track within the store.

As he tried on the second pair, the sales lady chimed in as if she had been a paid plant by adding, "I didn't start running until college and now it has become my social network and biggest hobby." Noah looked toward her cheery realm without responding. He laced up a brilliant royal blue pair this time and toured the store in another half-hearted trot. Thinking he couldn't possibly disagree, I pleaded, "Come on, Noah, to what degree do you admit that running track could have positive outcomes for you?" This time, he responded flatly, with only two words: "Thirty percent." I left the store with a hopeful smirk, brought on by his dry humor and those brilliant new royal blue running shoes.

Come spring semester, that thirty percent became one hundred: Noah attended every track practice. I performed private and silent celebratory dances in the kitchen each day after he returned. He set goals, got faster, and made those once new shoes become well worn. His jaunts around the track were not half-hearted...they were at full speed. Although no new friends were ever mentioned, he was off the sofa.

That same spring I was required to pay for repairs to a slightly damaged rented mermaid costume that Eli had worn to a party. The costume shop attendant said something close to, "Must have been some party!" I smiled and nodded, taking delight in handing over the extra 80 reales. Later that semester, I overheard a group of students in the senior hallway referring to a different gathering saying, "Eli wore a bathrobe and nothing else." Apparently a glimmer of his former confident and playful personality was returning in the form of pairing Timberland boots and a grey terry-cloth robe as party wear.

I have learned from experience how heart-wrenching it is to see unhappy children, but, thanks to Michael's grandmother, I no longer question how I will react: I will always take the joyful route, and hopefully my children will follow.

*Kimberly Russell is a native of Baltimore, Maryland, and teaches there currently. She has taught ESOL in Brazil, Peru and India for 8 years and in the U.S. for 15 years.*

# ACCIDENTAL STUNTMAN
## *Brent Wingers*

We had just finished playing a friendly game of futbol in a neighboring town thirty minutes from home. As the sun moved low in the sky, I realized we had played longer than anticipated, and this meant riding back as dusk fell upon the city. It would be a hurried departure, a race against the setting sun.

Shortly after arriving in Honduras, I had been fortunate enough to find a lifelong friend in a local PE teacher. We shared a common interest in motorcycles and a proclivity for adventure. My newfound comrade had recently purchased an on-road/off-road motorcycle. The bike was the epitome of cool, and I immediately followed suit and bought an identical one. Our friendship flourished and Sundays became our riding days, days when we would gear up and take off to wherever our fancies carried us. The motorcycle provided newfound mobility and access to the world outside my apartment. I careened through the streets of Honduras with a sense of invincibility, my true identity hidden safely behind a sleek gray helmet and recently purchased cowboy boots.

As the afternoon sun faded, I walked quickly toward my motorcycle while recalling the practical advice my father, the co-founder of a motorcycle club and lifelong rider, had given me: "Keep the rubber side down, wear decent boots, and never wear shorts." In my efforts to leave quickly and save precious daylight, however, I opted for the same sweaty t-shirt, spikes, and pair of shorts from the game.

Pure bliss best describes the riding of a motorcycle through the Honduran countryside. The landscape, people, and intermittent roadside Pepsi signs combine to elicit a sense of peace. Honduras itself is full of extremes. Some experience a place ridden with crime and drugs, with violence permeating all strata of society. Others, and I count myself among them, see unending beauty, generous and welcoming people, and a vibrant culture.

I remember driving fast. I can still feel the awkwardness of trying to shift gears with spikes on, along with the freedom of the wind whipping across my t-shirt and around my legs. It was a moment of true euphoria.

As darkness crept nearer, I didn't see it coming. From the divided highway, a Toyota pickup truck pulled directly out in front of me. My motorcycle instantly met the rear truck tire. The bruising on my legs would suggest I first hit the side of the truck bed around thigh level. I promptly flipped forward into the back of the pick-up, caught by the far side of the bed. I have resisted thinking about my fate should I have made it past the truck bed and onto the unforgiving pavement.

I was knocked out upon impact.

The next memory was of coming to in the bed of an unfamiliar pickup truck. I looked my body up and down, trying to assess where I was and what was happening. There was certainly blood, and I remember worrying about not wanting to see my own bones in disarray. I know enough about psychology and physiology to understand my next response, adrenaline. I snapped into focus, mind sharper than it has ever been, engaged in a singular task: survival.

The back window was tinted black and the truck was at a standstill. As I came to, my first reaction was that the driver might not even know I was in the truck. I scooted forward toward the cab and raised my now awkwardly out-of-place soccer cleat to the back window, gently tapping it to give my new acquaintances an idea of my continued existence.

The gentle "tap, tap, tap" on the back window was met with a most unexpected response. The truck tires squealed and the vehicle lurched forward into the night.

Was this truck really still driving with a freshly bloodied motorcyclist in the back?

Thirty yards ahead the truck braked abruptly and pulled over to the side, driving at a slow, leisurely pace for a few moments. About ten seconds later, I was met with another quick takeoff. The truck traveled another few hundred yards and then changed speeds and slowly drove along the roadside yet again. This process repeated, over about a mile, with the truck never reaching a full stop.

With the adrenaline still pumping, my mind calculated and assessed in a split second a situation I hadn't yet considered, even as a remote possibility. Many people carry handguns in Honduras, especially in vehicles. No one else was around, as far as I could tell, and the highway was not extensively travelled. Add to that the fact that more than a fair share of crimes go unsolved. If the truck occupants had a gun, using it might present an easier solution than swapping insurance details, paying hospital bills, or repairing a smashed motorbike.

The truck was following a pattern of slowing by the side and speeding up to send a message. When it slowed once again, I flung myself out of the pick-up and rolled into the ditch alongside the road. It was a healthy mix of anger and adrenaline that brought me to my feet as I unlatched my helmet and hurled it at the truck speeding away, spitting gravel from its back tires. I remember wanting the helmet to hit the window, but the vehicle was moving away from me too quickly, and it landed with a dull and unfulfilling thud on the pavement.

The hurt set in after the truck was out of sight. With sharp pains all over and blood mixing with the sweat of my t-shirt, I turned and began to wander back toward my bike. Friends who had played in the futbol game were now traveling along the same stretch of highway. They passed my laid-out motorcycle that people had dragged to the side of the road but didn't see anyone next to it. Driving past, they eventually came upon me, limping, bloodied, and ragged on the shoulder of the road. After staring in disbelief as I excitedly recounted the recent events, we were off to the hospital.

I had multiple cuts that were cleaned up, but thankfully no serious concussion and no broken bones. Even though the bruising had started on my legs and back, I was allowed to go home and sleep in my own bed, which was all I can really remember wanting.

In the days and weeks that followed, the story spread around school and amongst friends and family back home. There was a fleeting effort to find and locate the truck, as I had managed to remember the first three letters of the license plate. The attempt to find the truck involved a very wealthy and well-connected Honduran family, pistol-toting Russian twins, and a two-hour trip to a sweltering police station. Despite the efforts, no truck was found and no justice was to be had. Although I still seethed with anger about the experience, I was thankful to be alive.

Eventually, the motorcycle was fixed, an entirely new front half to replace the original. I was back riding after a few months, Sundays and otherwise. Faint scars remain on my legs to this day, and I still have some lower back issues that I attribute to that fateful night. My anger has long since been replaced by a sense of wonder—wonder as to why this accident occurred, and wonder at my good fortune to survive the whole incident.

*Brent Wingers, originally from Columbus, Wisconsin, taught in the U.S. for one year prior to moving abroad. He has since spent 11 years in the international teaching community. After nine years of teaching middle and high school social studies, he transitioned into administration and currently resides in Saudi Arabia. Brent has previously lived and taught in Honduras, Myanmar, and Indonesia.*

# FRIEND DRAFT
*Jay Goodman*

The friend draft begins the moment you first extend your hand. Name, where you're from, where you taught before, what you'll be teaching this time. They say the same things, but subbing in years at current school where you said last location. It's repeated so many times in the first week that it can begin to feel meaningless, like the safety video on a plane. But it's not meaningless. You're being evaluated, even if that evaluation is hiding behind a warm smile and a cold beer. These people are looking for new friends, friends to replace the ones lost to new schools at the end of June, friends to build out their book clubs and pickup basketball games and wine nights. But spots are limited. The draft matters.

It was my first Friday in Dalian, China. First week at a new school. And it was happy hour. They were established, seasoned veterans, and they were heading to a local bar, as they did every Friday from about 4-6pm, before retreating to their quiet fatherly lives. And I was invited. So I came home from school, put on my nicest white tee, made sure I was on time, and met them in the lobby. I got in the cab.

"You guys do this every Friday?"
"Yeah." Strong start.
"What beer have they got there?"
"They've got Devolution on tap."
"Yeah, I had their APA. Too hoppy. Anyone can make a beer taste good if you just jam it full of hops. But it's kinda a lazy way to make good beer, isn't it?"
"Devolution is Brandon's company." Brandon turned around from the passenger seat and waved.
"I probably just need to give it another try. Maybe I just had a bad pint."
"I personally test it anywhere it's served."
"Right. OK."

The bar was empty, and we took a spot upstairs. I ordered the APA. And when I finished, I ordered another one to prove how much I liked it. And then one was ordered for me.

"I love this beer. The hops are pretty bang-on," I said in Brandon's general direction. It was barely five o'clock and I was starting to lose the conversational plot, the floor beneath me becoming spongy and angular.

"What percentage is this?"
"About 7."
"That's what I thought. That's my favourite percentage."

Another one was ordered for me. I was deep into the tryout now and couldn't see my way out. I could barely see the door. I didn't know where I was or how to get home. Another pint, and then, finally, a cab. By the time it arrived, the subtle greens of the surrounding hills were spilled paint, and the lines on the road doubled up at a distance wide enough to create a new lane. I rolled down the window.

"You alright?"
"Fine."

I got my head almost all the way out before barfing five pints of 7% APA down the side of the cab. Thirty seconds later we pulled into our driveway. Yes, I was embarrassed, but the road to redemption was clear. I realized I'd inadvertently created a moment to impress these people with some quick thinking. I removed my t-shirt, wiped down the outside of the car and gave the driver the thumbs up. Definitely no problem here. I stepped into the building and got into the elevator. It stopped on the second floor. A woman stepped in, looked at me standing there topless, holding my vomit shirt, and turned away. "Xie, xie," I said, the Chinese for "thank you" being the only Mandarin I knew.

"You're welcome" she said, staring into the dull steel of the elevator door.

A minute later, I walked in my front door. My wife, Dani, looked at me with a face stuck somewhere between confusion and the knowledge that her reputation was going to need rehabilitation way too early in the year. "Oh no."

"Don't worry. I've got four new friends. They really like me," I said, closing the bathroom door and curling up on the cold tiles.

The draft starts in earnest in the second week when all the veterans have returned and someone hosts a house party. This was my wheelhouse. I'd been reading all summer, memorizing facts and anecdotes to impress people. I knew loose histories of nearby places, all the recent championship teams, the voting records of several members of congress, and half the chorus of all the potential "songs of summer." I was a one-man trivia team, designed to wow the crowds. The conversation, as it often does in those first pivotal days, floated towards travel.

"So, where are you guys thinking about going over the first break?" I asked.
"We're thinking Japan," Scott replied.
"That's awesome. They've got some weird stuff there. I really want to go."
"Yeah, I saw you can do Mario Kart on the streets of Tokyo."
"Yep, and they've got those sexbots."
"What?"
"Like these AI robots, but for sex. You know."
"I don't know. What are you talking about?"
"C'mon, you know. It's all over the news. They're AI, so they learn to love you."
"It's not all over the news. What do you do with them?"
"Well, they're sexbots."
"This doesn't exist."
"Look it up."
"I don't want that search on my phone."

When I got home later that evening, Dani looked up from her book.

"Were you talking about sexbots?"
"No, why?"
"Anna said you were, and it was weird."
"It wasn't weird."
"You just said you weren't talking about them."
"Well, it came up."
"Did you bring it up?"
"No."
"No?"
"It just sort of came up naturally. I don't think anyone knows who said sexbot first."
"Was it you?"
"I made three more friends."

The transition from newbie to veteran is a swift one. You go home for the summer, and when you return there are 35 new faces, 35 new names, 35 new stories, which is enough permutations to confuse even the most attentive of sexbots. Our soggy returning-staff brains don't stand a chance. But we have to try. Because this is the chance. There are 35 potential friends in front of us, and if you don't pick up the best ones, some other friend group is going to get them. Time is limited, you have to move fast.

"Kevin, some of us are getting beers after work, wanna come?"
"I'm Kyle."
"Sorry, you know how it goes with all the names. You in?"
"Actually, I don't drink."
"That's cool. We're getting Korean BBQ. Just come hangout."
"I'm a vegetarian."
"Grilled eggplant."
"I think you're trying to invite Kevin."
"No, Kevin and his wife said they were going out exploring tonight."
"That's Doug."
"Hmm. Anyway, wanna come?"
"No, I'm good. Thanks, though."
"Ok, see you at basketball on Wednesday."
"That's Kevin again."

I drafted no one that year.

Sometimes, though, there's no draft at all. The first contact with potential friends is often with the ones just as clueless as you are, at the gate in your "home of record," in the pickup bus from the airport, at the optional jet-lagged breakfast that is attended by everyone. Absent of the new-staff/returning-staff power dynamic, these moments are loaded with real potential. These are the friendships that will define, at minimum, your first few months. So it's important to get it right and to cut people as quickly as possible.

Against the cold shine of a streetlight, I could see the outline of his Ross Geller haircut. I could hear the way the "Os" in his words shifted into "Ahs." When someone switched on a light, I caught a glimpse of his shirt, which had a clock with twelve 5s on it ("it's five o'clock somewhere" was how he later, nonsensically, explained it to me). It was coming up on midnight, and we, as new staff, had all been collected at the airport and jammed onto a bus. We were tired, hungry, and confused and yet there he was, introducing himself to people, asking them questions about their family, helping them with luggage. There was nothing to like about any of this, and it all added up to an easy first cut.

I saw him again days later. It was the newbie party in someone's under-decorated house. The harsh Colombian fluorescent lights bounced off the tiles, casting dull shadows above and below everyone's eyes. J Balvin rattled out of a tinny bluetooth speaker, the kind you get free in a case of Bud, and I retreated to the kitchen to escape into another beer. The music changed. I opened my beer, tossed the cap in the garbage, and by the time I re-entered the party, there were twenty people moving in unison, Matt as their leader. Not being American, I didn't know that I was witnessing the Electric Slide. I did know I didn't like it, and I did know I didn't like Matt.

That year, I spent an evening tossing rotten fruit from my 20th story balcony into the woods below. Matt wasn't there. I spent a day riding a bus into the mountains to cook a pig. Matt wasn't invited. And when he and his wife invited me and my wife over for dinner, I faked malaria and had myself hospitalized for a week. But later, as my new friends developed new interests, or moved out of the city, I realized there was a hole in my friend roster. At this point, he was carrying with him a couple of strong character recommendations.

Some friendships happen quickly, like the time it takes to vomit out a car window. Some happen slowly and almost unconsciously. House parties of forty become dinners of fifteen become trips of six until eventually there you are watching the MLB preseason with someone who just months ago wore a t-shirt so stupid you declared any potential friendship an outright impossibility.

The balcony, his or mine, became our space, the kind you need when friends and siblings are continents away, deep in their own lives full of Sunday family dinners and ballet lessons and tax returns. What began as a single conversation turned into an ongoing one, occasionally punctured by the tragedy of dealing with tragedy from abroad. Later that year, my parents' marriage collapsed. Soon after, Matt's dad passed away. Through both, we sat in cheap patio chairs overlooking parking lots, the conversation growing even in silence.

And when we did leave the balcony, the conversation continued as we closed bars, as we got kicked out of a hot springs in Bolivia, as he officiated my wedding, and as we grossly realized neither of us had left a pool in the Philippines for over six hours. And it continued as I interviewed with his school in Shanghai, and as I got our apartment assignment, and as we realized our new balconies were thirty feet apart.

There's a distinct beauty to friendship abroad. It's quirky and bizarre and often involves the type of people that your life at home wouldn't touch. People with accents you barely understand, people who have lived places you can't pronounce, and people who irritate you for months before the constant rubbing of your lives together exposes some rich commonality. The draft matters. But only insofar as it helps you cut the people who insult your beer, or puke in cabs, or poorly navigate simple small talk. It's not a substitute for hours, real hours, the kind you only get when wearing a t-shirt that holds the clock still.

*Jay Goodman, originally from Toronto, currently teaches in Shanghai, China. He has taught high school for 13 years, 4 in Ontario and 9 abroad in Honduras, Colombia and China.*

# A BOX OF CHOCOLATES
## *Daniel Moraguez*

Living in Taiwan for me was truly like a box of chocolates. On any given day, I never knew what I was going to get. While not every personal encounter was positive or even pleasant, collectively they resulted in an amazing experience that made six years feel like six months.

Towards the end of a particularly trying school year, Mr. and Mrs. Lee paid me a visit.
"Mr. Moraguez, we are so grateful for everything you've done for our daughter Nicole this year."
"Mr. Lee, it's my job. You don't have to thank me. Really, it was my pleasure."
Mind you, Nicole once pooped inside a tent and blamed it on a bear while the class was on a camping trip.

"Regardless, we would like to invite you to dinner. We will pick you up this Friday evening."

"Thank you. That would be lovely."

They ended up taking me to their favorite sushi restaurant in Taipei. Gleaming wooden paneling, intimate lighting, and the smell of fresh wasabi greeted me along with the host. It was obvious they were regulars. The chef came out and introduced himself, we took our seats, and the meal began.

The chef presented each new dish with an explanation of its composition, preparation, and quality. It was quite a display, a ceremony even, and it went on for hours. Dish after dish. After dish. It was delicious (even the live sea urchin), but there was way too much of it. I had been full for a long time before I finally decided to say something. "Mr. Lee, how does the chef know when to stop?"

"Oh, Mr. Moraguez, don't worry! I called ahead and told him you were American. He knows you eat a lot."

Another time, someone I was seeing invited me to dinner at his sister's house in the southern part of the island. Although nervous, I agreed to go. The teenage nephews eagerly practiced their English. "Thank you. Where are you from?" they kept repeating. The gathering, awkward and tense at first, saw the nervousness dissipate once the alcohol started flowing. We butchered a few karaoke tunes. Justin Bieber's *Baby* and *Never Say Never* were popular with the nephews, but Wanting Qu's *You Exist in My Song* was the hit of the night. The only thing English about the song was the title. The singing was indeed painful— Simon Cowell wasn't going to be knocking on our door that night—but the laughter never seemed to end.

There was also the time I went with my friends Josh and Elise on a bike ride. Shortly after starting, Elise got a flat tire. An elderly Taiwanese man, wrinkled and with a cigarette dangling from his lips, came out of his house and offered to help. He did us the favor of pumping her tire. After saying a few thank yous and offering a bow or two, we were on our way. A few miles down the road, the tire went flat again. We decided to walk to the firehouse down the street and "ask" for directions to a bike repair shop. By "ask," I mean point and gesture. Instead of giving us directions, one of the firemen loaded the bike on the back of his truck and drove away with it...and Elise. While we waited, the other firemen served us hot tea, boiled peanuts, and "talked" to us about baseball: "New York Yankees...very good!"

There were times when the language barrier made even the simplest of tasks incredibly frustrating—calling a cab, doing laundry, ordering a meal, or paying bills to name just a few. For the first few months in Taiwan I kept confusing the tones for chicken and taxicab. I inadvertently kept asking for "chicken cars" and didn't understand why I was getting strange looks in return.

There were also those weird times when strangers asked to take a picture with me or called me handsome or told me I had beautiful eyes. Once I was trying to show a visiting friend Chiang Kai-shek Memorial Hall, one of the popular landmarks, and was approached by an elderly gentleman who insisted on taking our picture and chatting us up. "You embrace my dog," he ordered as he prepared his camera. Confused and uneasily holding his dog, my friend and I stood there for the picture.

When picking a piece from a box of chocolates, sometimes you get a flavor you like, a caramel or coconut, and sometimes you get something that tastes like medicine. The experience living in Taiwan taught me about tolerance, patience, and empathy. It taught me that my way isn't always the best way, that awkward or frustrating moments are often followed by good times, and that, like a box of chocolates, it's exciting not to always know what comes next.

*Daniel Moraguez, a native of Miami, Florida, is currently working on a Ph.D. in Education Leadership at the University of Virginia in Charlottesville. He taught 3rd -5th grade in Taiwan for 6 years and in New York City for 6 years.*

# BRAVE
## *Colleen McCabe*

As the savory scent of warm pork and ginger drifted through the air, a fellow American on the Shanghai dumpling tour turned to me and asked, "How did you become so brave and move overseas?"

It was a question I'd been asked many times before, but had always disregarded. This time the question made me stop and reflect, maybe because the questioner was a woman who had given birth to *triplet boys*. I think having *a* child is one of the bravest things a person can do. Entering into parenthood, despite all the books written on the topic and the fact that an overwhelming majority of the people who have walked this earth have experienced it, is quite possibly embarking into the greatest unknown. But it's often those friends with kids who wonder the most how I could do this and I just think, *You had kids! You're brave every day!*

That, to me, is the definition of bravery. Brave means putting others first no matter the cost. It's rarely as extreme as running into a burning building to save a stranger or loved one from the encroaching flames. Instead, it's usually about making big sacrifices on a daily basis in service of those you love or, in some cases, don't even know. My decision to move overseas, in comparison, doesn't feel selfless. Nor does it seem brave.

I certainly didn't feel brave at the airport the morning I was set to leave for Korea. I crumbled into my Mom's arms like an air dancer outside a car dealership. I sat outside the gate before boarding the plane blubbering over goodbye texts and heartfelt sentiments from friends and family. But once I was on that plane, the hard parts—the goodbyes—were behind me. I do recall, over the Pacific Ocean, momentarily thinking, *you're flying to a foreign country where you know no one.* But I didn't linger on the thought; I went back to my regularly scheduled inflight entertainment.

Arriving at Incheon Airport, I was greeted by a school staff member who drove me to my new digs. Two more met us at the apartment, giving a thorough "tour" of the ten-square-meter space, diligently leaving sticky notes on appliances and electrical equipment to help me know what every switch controlled. Then they left. All I had was a box of provisions (peanut butter, jelly, juice, bagels, milk), a calling card, a subway card, and my four suitcases. It was late; nighttime masked the reality that daylight would bring.

I woke up the next morning and gazed out the window of my 26th floor apartment. I noted the river nearby and the massive space-age building across the street. *A performing arts center? A conference hall?* I got to work unpacking the few bags in my possession. I called my family with that handy calling card. I started a list of organizational and kitchen items I would need to buy. Occasionally, I stopped for a snack from the provision box. I frequently stood at the window in the living room and just peered down, trying to orient myself in some way but not actually daring to *go outside* to do so. Cars were speeding by. Pedestrians migrated between the nearby subway station, department store, rows of office buildings, and the multitudes of restaurants and shops sitting right below me.

And that's when reality hit. I couldn't muster the courage to leave my apartment. The excitement of the move, the tears and hugs and goodbyes, the packing of all my earthly possessions into a couple of suitcases, the moving to a foreign country: I had conquered that. But this was uncharted territory. My brain had automatically categorized this differently from travel or a vacation. And now I was physically stuck.

I rationalized staying in my apartment in a lot of irrational ways: *I don't know the language. Where would I go? What if I got lost? The other newbies are probably holed up as well, just waiting for orientation day. These are your final days of summer, time to read, relax, and get over jet lag.* For 48 hours I lived my new life in Korea on the 26th floor, in my tiny one-bedroom apartment, sustaining myself on peanut butter and milk, looking down and around, taking "life" in and utterly scared to venture out alone.

The day before orientation was to begin, my principal called me and asked how I was doing. "Great!" I confidently declared. "Have you met any of the other newbies?" she inquired. *Huh? Aren't we all just spending these 48 hours sequestered to our apartments?* "Uh, well, no. I don't have anyone's contact number." She shared some phone numbers of new and returning staff, but as I hung up the phone, I realized I felt as paralyzed about the thought of cold-calling strangers as I did about stepping one foot out the door.

Luckily, a fellow newbie (and soon-to-be first friend in Korea) called me before I had to talk myself into any miracle moves. She invited me to Korean BBQ that night with a group of new and returning staff. "Meet us in the lobby!" she said, not knowing the only time I'd seen that lobby was the night I arrived, blurry-eyed and dazed. I opened my front door for the first time since arriving in Korea. I stepped over the threshold.

I took the elevator down the 26 floors and met my new friends.

*********

The woman who'd asked "How did you become so brave and move overseas?" was still waiting for my answer. In my mind, the decision to experience life in a new country paled in comparison to the courage to give birth to and take care of triplets. In her mind, leaving the comforts of home behind to move to a country where I knew not one soul nor one word of the language is the definition of bravery. Maybe bravery, like beauty, is in the eye of the beholder.

*Colleen McCabe, originally from Huntington Beach, California, teaches in Shanghai, China. She has taught elementary school for 13 years, 6 in the U.S. and 7 in South Korea and China.*

# THE FINGER
### *Gabrielle Clover*

A cluster of children huddled under the naked tree in the centre of the sandpit, digging through the layer of snow to the clammy granules below. Occasional shouts of "hey that's mine" or "give it here" were quickly hushed so the duty teachers wouldn't interfere. The sandpit was usually abandoned in the brisk Budapest winter, with children opting instead to build snowmen or play football in the slush.

The bell rang, echoing into the forest behind the school fence. They lined up in rows. Fifty-two nations represented by three hundred students. I stood on the bench so I had a clear view, everyone's breath visible as they waited for me to speak. "Good morning, students. Vlad, a secondary student, has lost a finger."

There was a collective gasp.

"A fake finger," I clarified. "If anyone has Vlad's finger, you need to *hand* it in."

Sniggers rippled through the teachers.

"The reward for finding the finger will be a voucher for the bookshop."

Silence.

"Or a block of chocolate?" I offered.

Murmurs of approval.

"Can it be candy if you are allergic to chocolate?" called a voice from the back of year two.
"I guess so."
"Can we choose the flavour?" someone else asked.
"Yes, as long as the finger is returned unharmed."

I couldn't believe that I was negotiating for the safe return of a prosthetic finger with a bunch of primary school students.

Vlad, an atypically brash eighth-grader, had lost two fingers in less than a year, and both on the school playground. He lost the first, his real finger, in a terrible accident on April Fools Day, which somewhat delayed the treatment of his injury. He was trying to retrieve a soccer ball and climbed the fence. As he jumped down, a ring he was wearing caught and tore his flesh from the bone. He stumbled through the playground screaming, "Ambulance, call an ambulance!" His friends laughed, "Just get the ball!" Vlad kept screaming, both hands held in front of him, blood streaming down his forearm.

"It's past 12:00. You can't prank anymore," yelled Mrs. Peters.

Vlad ran towards the school building.

"You can't go in without a toilet pass!" She waved the blue pass at him. He ran in anyway. Mrs. Peters stormed off after him, fishing around in her coat pocket for her detention slips. As she got closer to the door, she saw the red trail of splotches. Vlad was near the entrance with Mr. Lockier, the PE teacher, who happened to be walking by on his way to warm up some spaghetti bolognese for lunch. "Call the ambulance!" shouted Mr. Lockier, lifting Vlad's blood-soaked hand.

Mrs. Peters took out her phone, dialing 112 as she ran past them towards the nurse's office. Multitasking was something she was unaccustomed to and she slipped on a small puddle of blood. Her phone hit the wall just before her head hit the ground and she became Casualty Number Two.

Mr. Lockier swore for the first time since he had watched his son being born three years before. He grabbed the first student he could find. It happened to be Seoyoung, a painfully shy Korean student who sat by herself near the lockers to minimise the possibility of human interaction during lunch. "Get the nurse!" She stared back at him, eyes wide with fear and confusion.

"NURSE! GO!"

She trundled off, hands flapping like a stranded seal.

The nurse came running and went immediately to Mrs. Peters, who was lying semi-conscious in a pool of blood. "What did you do?!" the nurse shouted at Vlad, who looked like he had been apprehended by Mr. Lockier, literally red-handed.

Vlad whimpered.

"It's Vlad, his hand." The nurse looked up and saw Vlad giving her the finger, albeit a bloody and bony one. She swore for the first time since stepping on her daughter's lego at breakfast that morning.

He was taken away in the ambulance, and after hearing the same opinion in four hospitals—in Hungary, Slovakia and Austria—the parents finally consented to the finger being amputated. A prosthetic finger, one which cost the same as my annual salary, was fitted in Russia. It was this finger that he later lost during an illicit snowball fight with a group of tenth-grade girls. It was this finger I was trying to buy back from the children with chocolate.

The finger was eventually placed on my desk, in a box like something out of *The Godfather*. It was still covered in sand, having presumably been buried for safekeeping in the sandpit.

Accompanying the finger was a note:
> Returned by 5B
> Izabella - Dairy Milk
> Gareth - Twix
> Jiwoo - Skittles
> Kelly - Gummy bears
> And so on…

*Gabrielle Clover is originally from New Zealand and started her teaching career in the outback of Australia, where her students had a pet crocodile called Mr. Bombastic. She has been teaching for 7 years internationally. She made her way to Slovakia via Norway and Mongolia in spite of her pathological fear of the cold.*

# INSTANT FRIENDS IN A FOREIGN LAND
*Lindsey T. Murff*

After almost a decade of marriage, four kids, two vehicles, and a house with a pool, it was time to completely change our lives and our teaching careers and leave the comforts of our lifelong home. Goodbye Texas; hello, China! Early on, we made the decision that we would not live with a foot in each place. If Shenzhen, China was going to be our new home, then it was time to jettison it all and make the leap of faith. The "For Sale" sign went up in our front yard and in our vehicles' windows. There were numerous garage sales and for-sale posts on Craigslist. Our whole life had to fit into twelve suitcases and six carry-ons...and stay under the allotted weight limit.

Finally, it was the morning of our very last garage sale. It all had to go! People were showing up in our yard before we were even ready. Cash was changing hands and our things were finding new homes. We had an odd feeling of liberation, but it was the little things leaving our possession that made us most nostalgic and a bit sad. A tiny wheelbarrow that used to sit on our mantel as a fall decoration was carried to a stranger's car. It was more than a wheelbarrow: it held memories of our children sitting near the fireplace, posing for pictures with all of the fall decor. That little wheelbarrow held the scent of potpourri and fireplace aromas. It represented all we had known and all the things we cherished. Were we making the right choice?

As our sale dwindled down to the miscellaneous—a pair of oven mittens, three mismatched plates, a bag of yarn, Christmas wrapping paper, a hammer, a bent kite, an over-loved stuffed animal, and a few other odds and ends—the customers began to slow. A gentleman approached and kindly asked if we would mind donating whatever didn't sell to the local high school to use in their own fundraiser. It all had to go, so of course I agreed. As he loaded his car, we got to talking about how we were selling it all to teach abroad in China. His eyebrows shot to the top of his forehead, and I could read the judgement behind his eyes. "China, eh?" he said as he looked up at our big house and scratched his head. Just like all of our friends and family, he too thought we were crazy. I shrugged and said aloud what he wouldn't, "Yes, we are probably a little crazy." A nervous laugh confirmed what his face was saying. We made a little more small talk before he drove off with the last of our possessions.

A deep breath and an empty house. A chapter had closed. All that was left to do was wait for the big day to fly out, but a week later, I heard a knock on the door. The same gentleman had returned.

He looked as though he was searching for words. I greeted him kindly, but honestly, I was confused. "Ma'am, you know how you were telling me that you all are moving to China to teach over there? Well, the oddest thing just happened. Another family, just a few blocks away, was also having a garage sale. They, too, donated their things. Well, ma'am, they said that they are also moving to China. Now, I don't know where in China or if they are also teachers, but I just thought it was the oddest thing that I would meet two families within a week, both moving to China. So, I don't know what you'll do with this, but here's their phone number." He placed the scrap of paper in my hand and walked away after wishing me a good day.

How weird! What are the odds? What should I do now? Do I call a complete stranger or throw this number away?

I did what any curious person would do. I went to the phone and called a complete stranger, and then it was me trying to search for words. I fumbled through the greeting but then got straight to the point. "Um, hi. You don't know me, but we just had a garage sale because we are moving to China. Apparently, the same guy that picked up our garage sale donations also picked up from you? He gave me your phone number. You're moving to China, too? You probably never heard of the city before, but we're moving to a huge city of twelve million called Shenzhen." My heart pounded, waiting for the response on the other end.

"Shut up! No way! That's where we're going, too!"

It didn't take long for us to realize that we were both moving to China, to the same city, and to the same exact school. They were teachers too! We had both interviewed with the same person, on the same day, both getting teaching offers in Shenzhen with the same school...and we lived less than a mile from each other in Houston. Needless to say, it took no time at all for our families to meet. We spent the final days of summer before the big move together, meeting up for dinners, sharing our experiences with the Chinese visa process while continuing to reference our astonishment at the connection.

On the first day of new teacher orientation, 8,000 miles away from Houston, we quickly found each other and embraced out of relief and joy. We navigated our new city together, getting lost on more than one occasion while learning the ins and outs of a city with more people than Houston, Dallas, Fort Worth, San

Antonio, and Austin combined. And, as fate would have it, we also became teachers to each other's children.

I always say that it takes a year before a new place begins to feel like home. It takes a year of building new traditions for things to feel familiar. Our instant Texas friends helped us build China into a home before the requisite twelve months. We knew whom to turn to during both the good and the difficult times. Some traditions from home, like celebrating Thanksgiving, were shared together. The adventure of hunting for certain hard-to-find ingredients in a foreign land to prepare the holiday meal strengthened the bond of our families. The synchronous food comas following the turkey and dressing and cranberry sauce reminded us of days gone by. We were stuffed and satisfied with the comforts of our former home while still happy with the decision to sell our possessions and see what the world has to offer.

The moment I picked up that phone in Houston and called that stranger was the moment I knew for sure we had made the right choice, that it would all be okay. And, with the help of instant friends in a foreign land, it has been.

*Lindsey T. Murff, a native of Houston, Texas, teaches in Almaty, Kazakhstan. She has taught lower elementary for 14 years, 7 in Texas, 4 in China, and 3 in Kazakhstan. She is married to her best friend and has 4 children, as well as 3 fur babies. To learn more about her adventures abroad, visit; www.murffbunch.wordpress.com*

# ¿HABLAS ESPAÑOL?
*Cailin Minor*

The exchange was pleasant and dull, its road a familiar walk. All the landmarks were there, letting me know exactly where we would end up. He leaned in and smiled as he ushered us along the worn conversational path. "So, where are you from?" he asked. "The United States, Minnesota," I answered, shifting slightly in my seat. I paused, ready for my usual follow up response of "Near Chicago," but he seemed not to need the clarification. "Why are you traveling to Colombia?" he asked, curiosity written on his face. "I live there actually, I'm a teacher. I work in Medellín." His eyes lit up in surprise, clearly not the response he expected. His gaze shifted beyond me as he paused to accept his drink from the flight attendant's outstretched hand. I took the opportunity to ask where he was from, finding out we both live in the "City of Eternal Spring." "How long have you lived in Colombia?" he countered, sipping his soda. "Five years," I mumbled, bracing myself for his response. "Wow, five years! ¿Hablas Español?"

I hesitated, as I always do, when faced with this question. Two simple words that hang heavy for me. The question is asked with good intentions, and the asker always expects a simple response. Like the way your eager Aunt Barb asks if you're trying to have a baby yet, or questions your 37 year-old cousin about whether she's seeing anyone (damn it Barb, read the room. I'm on my third glass of wine and if Karen was seeing someone she would have brought him to the BBQ). The inquiry into my language abilities has always been a loaded question and one I dread answering. The answer isn't simple: I am not fluent nor am I a beginner. I am somewhere in the dreaded middle on the continuum of fluency. For all you teachers out there, if you graded me on a scale of 1-5, with 5 being fluent, I would be a 3.5. The simple answer that people are looking for, "Sí" or "No," never seems to get across the complexity I feel. How can I express the journey of learning another language and the experiences of frustration, pride, embarrassment, and accomplishment in one word? How was I going to answer this time?

I started to mentally weigh my options as I looked into his expectant face and sized up my seat partner. He was from Medellín, so his Spanish accent would be familiar, which is helpful. But he would probably speak really fast if he's not used to conversing with people whose first language isn't Spanish. Unfortunately, I was not fluent enough to explain my complex level of near fluency, nor did I think he cared to hear it. I could say "Sí," knowing the gamble was in what he said next. I've been in more situations than I care to admit where, after responding with a confident "Sí!," I didn't understand the very next sentence the person said and had to sheepishly repond, "¿Qué?" What's even worse is when I answer "Sí!" and then falter so much in the immediate exchange that the person switches back to English. They never say anything, or call me out on it, they just casually switch over. But the failure is palpable, and you have to live with the knowledge that this person found conversing with you painful enough that they would rather endure the conversation in their second language than listen to you butcher their mother tongue. In these situations, I am fully aware that my enthusiasm for the language far outweighs my skills. Although answering "No" was the safest option for my ego I knew it was the coward's way out. By downplaying my skills I would be missing out on the chance to enjoy the fruits of my language labors.

I gave him a hesitant smile and replied, "Sí, un poco," with as much confidence as if he asked me if I understood aerospace engineering. He read into my lackluster response and nodded, responding with something simple in Spanish. I was about to follow up when the flight attendant reappeared, stretched her arm out across me, and handed the man a small bag of pretzels. I seized the momentary distraction, grabbed my book, and retreated into reading. My uncertainty was weighing heavy, tipping the scales into not continuing the conversation in Spanish. The man seemed fine with the move, confirming his acceptance by pulling his headphones over his ears. I peeked sidelong at him as he settled in to watch a movie, content as he popped a pretzel into his mouth. I slumped a little in my chair. I sold myself short in my language abilities and once again passed up an opportunity to converse with someone in Spanish. To not only practice this language that I had enjoyed learning, but to also meet someone new. His laughter filled the space as he watched the movie. My mood darkened as I chided myself for my lameness.

Maybe I was still gun-shy after my most recent interaction with the Miami customs agents. Seemingly everyone in the Miami airport spoke Spanish; sometimes it felt more like South America than the US. Nothing had tested my Spanish confidence more than speaking with a stern Miami customs agent. The interaction usually went like this:

Me: (approach customs agent, palms already sweating)
Agent: (tone abrupt and unfriendly) *Where are you coming from?*

Me: *Colombia*
Agent: *What were you doing in Colombia?*

Me: (voice quiet, eyes downward) *I live there.*
Agent: (eyes me, then curtly, more like a statement than question) *¿Hablas Español?*

Me: (visibly sweating, my response like a nervous child called on in front of the class) *Sí*
Agent: *¿Cuál es su ocupación?* (What is your job?)

Me: (I am so uncomfortable that my statement now sounds like a question) *¿Profesora?*
Agent: (raises an eyebrow, suspicious as to why I am unsure of my job) *¿Hace cuánto que vive en Colombia?* (How long have you lived in Colombia?)

Me: (I know he finds me suspicious but I can't stop making my voice inflect) *¿Cinco?*
Agent: (rolls his eyes and sighs) *Go.*

The questions were simple enough but the interrogation style made me feel like I was new to speaking Spanish. I knew I couldn't let those interactions keep me from conversing with others.

I had put a lot of time and effort into studying over the past five years and had made some solid language gains. There were a few years of Saturday morning classes with Beatrice, a stern and stylish woman in her 60s we lovingly called "B-money" (never to her face). B-money was always slightly exasperated that you could not master one simple language when she had mastered three. Her favorite move was to force us to role-play mock scenarios as casual people around town; ordering food at a restaurant, checking in at the airport, and calling for a taxi. My husband and I thought we could "excel" in these scenarios by being easy patrons who only ordered water at restaurants and were happy for the taxi to pick us up at any time. B-money was not impressed.

There were countless Spanish podcasts to develop listening skills, apps to practice grammar, articles to read, and even a couple of tv shows too. If you are ever in the mood to travel the world with lawyer Raquel Rodriguez as she solves a mystery for a dying man, I highly recommend "Los Destinos" for your viewing pleasure. And finally, a year of group classes with colleagues. These sessions focused on practicing conversation, exponentially improving my skills except for the times we tried discussing the intricacies of social issues. We approached these issues with about as much intellect and subtlety as a drunk man or a toddler, or a drunk toddler. "When the Earth gets too hot that will be bad for us," we mused. "Yes, a hot Earth is bad for people AND animals." Groundbreaking.

But all the work and ups and downs had led to many great exchanges. My husband and I were able to comfortably travel around South America, enjoying new countries while speaking Spanish with people in cities and in the countryside. I also loved how much I was able to converse with coworkers at my school. Sometimes our meetings went back and forth between English and Spanish; I felt so much pride at being able to keep up in those conversations. I thought about some of our Colombian friends and how speaking in their native tongue allowed us to connect on a different level. I also considered the compliments I had received from friends and strangers on my Spanish once I opened up and let go of the fear of making mistakes.

My eyes wandered again towards the man sitting next to me, who was still engrossed in what was happening on the screen in front of him. I knew I had missed the window...the opportunity had passed. Maybe I could muster up the courage to engage in conversation after his movie was finished. There might be a second chance at showing off my skills and befriending my seatmate. I turned back to start reading and scowled at the book in my hands; a social savior for me but also a barrier and a crutch. I put down the book, no longer in the mood to read. I looked around at the other passengers chatting away in Spanish and felt a pang of jealousy.

I didn't know if I would ever get to the point where I could confidently proclaim "Sí!" when someone asks me that question. But I guess that is the dream, to truly feel like I could own the title of "bilingual." I knew to get there I would have to find a way to overcome my social language anxieties; to get comfortable with being uncomfortable.

I was still lost in my thoughts when her voice lilted, "¿Pollo o carne?" I was so distracted by my musings I didn't see the flight attendant sneak up on me. She loomed above, her hands perched on the sides of the food cart, waiting for my response. I blinked, trying to bring myself back to the current moment, and the buzz of passengers around me getting ready for dinner. She quickly noted my hesitation and read the slightly confused look on my face. I looked up at her, mouth poised to respond, when she tilted her head slightly and said, "¿Hablas Español?"

*Cailin Minor, a native of Burnsville, Minnesota, is a Literacy Coach in Shanghai, China. She has taught K, 1st, and 3rd as a homeroom teacher, and is in her second school as Literacy Coach. She has worked in an elementary setting for 12 years in South Korea, Thailand, Colombia, and China.*

# A SOFRA LOVE AFFAIR
*Charaine Poutasi*

My love affair began when I left the old city, taking my only possessions: a few pieces of kitchenware and a *sofra*, a Turkish rug used only for meals. The prediction of the captain's mother, that I would meet a stranger and fall in love and stay in Turkey, had come true. But that stranger didn't walk and talk; he didn't buy me flowers nor take me to dinner. That stranger was the *sofra*.

Whichever form a *sofra* is, it brings together a group of people at the end of a day to sit, chat, and eat a meal together. The *sofra* reminds me of meals back home in Samoa and New Zealand, where we would sit on the floor on woven mats and dine together, sometimes with only family and other times with church members, friends, or visitors passing by. The sound of laughter and music would compete with the din of clanging pots and pans, mothers shouting over the symphony of noises to make sure the steaming buns didn't overstay their welcome in the huge pot and that the right amount of garlic and ginger found their way into the chop suey. Food was always shared, never eaten alone.

This is a similar theme I see when at a Turkish home: women gathered around a stove, talking and cooking, sharing their food, sharing their woes, their joys, their life stories. The woven mats of Samoa, the woven rugs of Turkey—these are the settings where life is best lived. Perhaps it's the close proximity to the ground, everyone sitting in a way that makes getting up a challenge instead of a simple maneuver. Whatever it is, these settings weave people together, pulling each person closer, thread by thread.

My mother spent hours upon hours preparing dishes served in enormous bowls, always leaving enough for the visitors to take home. She was my mentor in the kitchen, teaching me that, despite the humongous portions, it really isn't so much about the amount of food you cook, but the way love is imparted into the recipes. I was once told by a Turk that I "cooked like a Turkish woman," asking where I had acquired such good cooking skills. My Samoan mother, a woman who never made it anywhere within an eight-hour time difference of Turkey, was unquestionably the secret to my success.

In Istanbul, I try to follow her example, inviting people to come together on the *sofra*, sharing my food and home with my new family away from New Zealand. Even when the menu has neither traditional Turkish nor Samoan fare—salmon blinis, gourmet pizzas, etc.—people still recline on the ground, exchanging stories and food, trials and tribulations.

But the *sofra* is not just something found in the comfort of one's own home.

During every summer, the beautiful artisan village Gümüşlük, in southwest Turkey, fills with boats and visitors on holiday retreats. It's where I've escaped to every year. At the restaurant Mimoza, tucked away next to the sea, the water laps at your feet as they sink in the sand. From the moment you walk in, you know you will be here for hours. You can breathe deep and fall in love with the idea that life really can be tranquil at times, a fact often forgotten when living in a megacity of over fifteen million. White tables, blue glazes on the crockery, and pink bougainville lure you into summer luxury. The same waiter in his pristine white shirt and jeans has been selling the tray of delights from the restaurant's menu for the decade-plus I have been coming. He remembers me every time. The price is high but the conversations with each group I travel with are even more rich.

Here, in Gümüşlük, the *sofra* does not need walls. There, in Istanbul, the *sofra* doesn't need the sea.

What is needed are the sweet smells, the tastes, and the people. There have been many changes to my foreign *sofra* community with the cycle of friends that have come and gone over my eleven years in Turkey. One thing that has not changed is how the *sofra* slows down life and recalibrates our priorities. Another thing that has not changed is how it keeps the memory of my mum with me. Her passion for cooking and for life, seen so clearly each time we gathered on the floors in Samoa and New Zealand, is now my passion. The beauty of how a meal can be shared with friends, instill memories of people, language, and culture, and impart a sense of family, is a big reason I have fallen in love with this place I now call my home.

Istanbul, relationships, food, and my mum: all four are woven into my own *sofra*, thread by precious thread.

*Charaine Poutasi is a New Zealand-born Samoan, originally from the deep south, Invercargill. Charaine teaches and resides in Istanbul, Turkey. She has taught in Early Years for the past 29 years. 11 years in NZ, 4 in the UK, 2 in Ukraine, and 12 in Istanbul, Turkey.*

# DRINKING MATE WITH CHECHO
*Larissa Nelson*

It is 8:00 in the morning and it's time to get up and milk the goats. I roll out of my lumpy cot bed in the attic of a small yellow house in the south of Chile and pull on my sweatpants, the cleanest shirt I can find, and my sheep's wool hat. It is a gray February day in the Southern Hemisphere summer and I pull on a fleece sweater while stumbling down the stairs, greeting my housemates.

We shuffle out of the crooked house by the edge of the stream, young people in our early to mid-20s yawning and joking: two boys from England, a French girl, a guy from Minnesota, and me, a small town girl from Idaho, on our way to meet Checho down at the goat house.

We are all volunteers through the World Wide Organization of Organic Farms (WWOOF) but in various stages of our lives; I am a veteran international school teacher on holiday, the

English boys have just finished uni, French girl is taking a gap year before her studies, and Lord knows what Jimmy is doing with his life—he certainly doesn't have a clue.

The farm is owned by a man named Matias, but he rarely makes an appearance. The day-to-day operations of the farm are managed by a man named Checho. He is the man kneeling next to us, calmly and patiently instructing us in the proper way to milk a goat, cracking a partially toothless grin when we struggle to make even a drop of milk fall into the plastic bucket. After milking the goats, we divide into two groups, half going to the small hut where a round of cheese will be made from the milk, and the other half heading back to the yellow house to start cooking breakfast, carefully cradling a small jar of fresh milk for the morning's coffee as the gray skies turn darker.

On a day like this, with the rain beginning to pour as we arrive to the cabin, we know to expect a lazy day ahead. When the weather is good, Checho has us making raised garden beds, repairing the green house, harvesting potatoes, packing up a hundred head of lettuce to sell at the market, or installing an electrified fence to separate the baby goats from their mothers. But on rainy days when there isn't much that can be done, Checho leaves what to do up to us WWOOFers. If we're especially motivated, we hitchhike our way into town to buy groceries and use the internet. However, on most days, we simply while away the hours inside, staying warm and dry while rain replenishes the farmland.

The best thing about rainy days on the farm is sitting around the old fashioned wood stove and drinking *mate* with Checho. For the uninitiated, mate (pronounced mah-tay) is a loose leaf herb that is served hot like tea with the water being consumed by using a thick metal straw with a filter on the bottom end to prevent the herbs from reaching your mouth. It has an earthy, almost bitter taste to it and contains a mild level of caffeine. In southern South America it's a social drink where a communal cup is passed around, each person taking a turn by drinking the entire cup, then passing it back to the one in charge of the hot water kettle. That person then refills it and passes it to the next person, straw pointing politely towards the receiver. Unlike most drinks, a specific etiquette is involved. Checho instructed us in the proper way to drink mate as we sat around on those rainy afternoons, telling stories and sharing about our lives.

We were all learning how to speak and understand Chilean Spanish with varying degrees of success. Often our conversations with Checho would be like a linguistic jigsaw puzzle, with everyone translating the part of the story they thought they understood, then piecing it together to create a verbal picture. Patagonian Spanish is both lilting and clipped, Checho's words flowing out in a sing-song rhythm that rose and fell with every sentence, the valleys and peaks of his intonation swallowing vowels and the crucial endings of words. As we put Checho's stories together in bits and fragments, we began to piece together what an incredible person he was.

He told us about how he never met his father, and how he lived with his grandparents while his mother found work up north in the capital. Checho would go out on the fishing boat with his Grandpa and, at the age of eight, became the boat's cook when their regular cook became ill. He described how the boat would rock back and forth so much that he would light two burners on the stove top, suspend the pot above the burners, and cook the food as it swayed back and forth.

It was the sea that saved them when soldiers came, "looking for weapons" Checho said, rolling his eyes. "We were farmers and fishermen in the campo," he said, "we had no weapons and were not rebellious." But the soldiers came anyway, killing livestock and slitting open bags of food, letting the flour run out, and leaving the produce to spoil.

"If it hadn't been for the food we were able to get from the ocean," Checho told us, "I don't know how we would have survived."

He told us about how he had built his own house, cutting down the trees in the forest, taking them to the sawmill to be processed into boards, and working every weekend for two years until his house was done. Checho seemed embarrassed to admit that it had taken him two whole years, and he emphasized that he only had the weekends to work, you see. It was during the telling of this story that we discovered Checho was practically illiterate. None of us understood the Spanish word for sawmill, and when we asked him to look it up in our Spanish-English dictionary, he refused to look at the book or write the word. I wrote the word on a piece of paper and he simply nodded his head in agreement despite, as we would later find out, how badly I had misspelled it.

In the following days we learned that Checho never really attended school, the educational system in Chile having been interrupted with Pinochet's rise to power and with his family's need for him to work from an early age.

It was during these conversations, passing the mate cup back and forth, listening and learning, that I began to truly understand the many incredible ways there are to be intelligent and useful in this world. Here I was, a college educated teacher, bilingual, well-traveled, reading Dostoevsky's *Crime and Punishment* for fun, and I was almost completely useless in this world I had brought myself to.

The other young people living with me on this farm were like me—millennials who knew what our favorite order was at Starbucks, how to bank online, the best day of the week to purchase international airline tickets (Tuesday), and yet, despite all our collective world knowledge, not one of us knew how to make bread. Or the best way to grow tomatoes. Or how to fix a tractor engine. Or when to separate baby goats from their mothers. And certainly none of us were capable of building our own house, from timber we had cut down ourselves, even if we had all the days of the week and all the years in a lifetime to work on it.

A month on this farm, working side by side with this man, reminded me time and time again how my skills and my knowledge base were relevant only to a particular culture and environment; a particular set of schema that was thousands of miles away from where I currently was, figuratively and literally.

This was never more apparent than when Checho walked into our little house to discover me up to my elbows in sticky bread dough, surrounded by my house mates. When we explained we were trying to make bread, he opened his eyes wide in surprise: "You all don't know how to make bread?!" he asked incredulously, shaking his head when we sheepishly admitted that we did not.

With that he pulled his blue knit sweater over his head, hung it up behind him and turned to face us, rolling up his sleeves. "OK then," he said, "let me teach you how to make bread."

There was nothing this man could not do when it came to growing plants, building things, taking care of animals, or managing the farm. Checho was extremely capable in his world, respected in his community and by his employer. There were times, sitting around drinking mate on those rainy afternoons, or out working in the garden, when we were shocked to discover something that Checho did not know; something about current events, a well-known pop icon or world leader, a famous international landmark or book. There was so much that he had no understanding or awareness of. And he wasn't really that interested to find out. I can't fault him for it either—there's really no satisfactory explanation for the Kardashians.

After my holiday I returned to a beautifully furnished apartment in the middle of Santiago, with its Wi-Fi and running hot water, a working fridge, and my king-size bed, but I carried with me from that farm a deep appreciation for the Chechos of the world. As our world moves more and more into this digital chaos, with emphasis placed on the number of likes you receive and how many followers you have and who you're wearing, let us remember and celebrate the people who know how to do truly useful things—the men and women who sow the seeds, grow the food, construct the buildings, fix the machines, milk the goats, and bake the bread. For the people who know how to cut down trees with their own two hands and make houses for real families to live in, and who know the value of a rainy day spent indoors talking with friends around a wood stove, sharing a cup of mate.

*Larissa Nelson, originally from Coeur d' Alene, Idaho, teaches in Shanghai, China. She has taught preschool for 7 years in Chile and in China.*

# FROM EGYPT TO MANILA: A JOURNEY OF A THOUSAND LIGHT YEARS
*Nicole Gough*

"Excuse me, miss, can I have a rubber?"

"A what?" I replied, turning to face an earnest-looking Egyptian student.

It had been a few months since I'd moved to Cairo, my first stint abroad, but each day brought new and amusing misunderstandings. That morning, for instance, someone had stolen the internet cord from the street outside, which might have derailed my lesson if I had actually had a computer in my classroom. But this was what international teaching was like, I told myself.

My students sat, notebooks open, pencils at the ready, awaiting my response.
"A rubber?" I repeated.

Ali in the front row pointed to his friend's eraser for emphasis: "A *rubber!*"

This was new—and I loved it. I loved that I was teaching in a school where laptops were absent and students drew lines on their paper with rulers and pencils. I loved writing my lesson plans by hand. I loved that, at the end of each lesson, the bell was rung manually by a hall matron. When I'd decided to teach overseas, I knew I'd be crossing time zones, but I hadn't realized I'd also be going back in time.

I couldn't be happier. Don't get me wrong. I'm not a laptop-destroying Luddite bent on wreaking havoc against Apple products and NASA. If it weren't for technology, I wouldn't be typing this or texting my sister photos of dried mango balls. The reality is, technology and I don't understand each other.

Technology is like a foreign exchange student from Mars who speaks in blips and wows its host family, while I'm the small child who accidentally gets spaghetti in the Martian's circuits, breaks it, and everyone hates me. I'm afraid of breaking the technology.

In all of this, Egypt was my accomplice. Together we hid from Instagram and high-speed internet streaming. My students said "rubber." I'd stockpile rubbers until the end of time if it meant never having to touch a projector.

Four years later, I accepted a job in Manila. How exciting it would be, I thought, to learn what students in the Philippines called erasers. I envisioned myself teaching in a small school on one of the Philippines' 7,107 islands, wiping chalk dust off my sleeves.

How wrong I was. Days after I signed my contract, technology found me, and it wasn't pretty. It started with friendly emails from my new colleagues, which seemed harmless until they started "inviting" me to do things like view documents and PowerPoints and items that are stored in mysterious intangible places like drives and clouds. Prior to that, I only ever got invitations to birthday parties and weddings, and that was fine by me. But no. My new school was full throttle into the cloud-powered future, and it was either jump on board or fall to the wayside to be eaten by feral people wielding book socks and manual-crank pencil sharpeners.

Arriving in Manila, my school provided tech workshops led by a fantastic IT guru, but I was miles behind my peers. *Miles.* They'd all zoomed off in their George Jetson flying cars, and I was still fording the river in my Conestoga wagon. In Egypt, I could rely on a power outage to get me out of using my SmartBoard. My school in Manila wanted me not only to use my SmartBoard, but to calibrate it by myself. I was terrified.

I know what you're going to say. "Oh, you're exaggerating. I'm sure you know more than you let on!"

My answer to you is a thump on the head with my woolly-mammoth-slaying club.

Our first session, a simple and entertaining lecture on how to use Google Drive, involved my colleagues soaring through their Google sites on their little Polly-Pocket-sized Macbooks while I poked at the mouse rectangle.

"Where do you prefer to store files over 10GB, in Google Drive or Hapara's Magical Hat? And why?"
"Will these files sync automatically to the Nimbus software in my home entertainment system?"
"How do you scroll on this machine?"

I'll let you guess which one was me, and no, I'm not kidding.

While our IT technician was friendly and helpful, I'm certain he thought I was a troglodyte that the director dragged out of a cave as part of a funny experiment.

"Sorry to bug you again, but I don't know how to find Power School."

"Cool...you don't know how to log in?"

"No, I know how to log in. I don't know how to get to the website." I then grunted and slouched off to discover agriculture.

But it wasn't limited to computers. Early in my first year in Manila, this conversation happened:

"My locker isn't working," said a student.

"Oh? Is it one of those electronic ones?"

"Yeah."

"In my day, we had combination locks."

That's right. I said *In my day*. Because I don't understand these young whippersnappers and their weird gadgets.

A few days later, the grade 10 curriculum leader sent an email asking if any of us knew where to locate the Google folder that housed a poem we were about to introduce. Eager to prove myself, I scoured Google drive for the entirety of my prep period before my email pinged through a message from Preston: he'd found it! But how!? Google Drive felt like a giant pond and the documents clever fish, and I was an emaciated participant in *Naked and Afraid* and my colleagues were Ewan McGregor in *Salmon Fishing in the Yemen*. I opened Google Drive and found NOTHING, while Preston found it right away—and I'll bet he was teaching while doing it, or sleeping, or finding John Gotti's body.

It was only a matter of time before the superintendent walked in to find me chiseling my notes on a stone. I had to do something to prove to them—and myself—that I could use technology without setting the school back a few thousand dollars. The time came in March, when I needed to record my students' end-of-semester presentations using an iPad. Ok, I thought, I can do this. Here in Manila, my students were writing code and winning Southeast Asian robotics competitions. Surely I could press "record" on an iPad.

On the day of the presentations, I felt ready. I had prepared by not sleeping the night before so I could list every possible catastrophe in my head. I had procured a fancy little clicker device that would allow students to move through their presentations without me stationing another student behind my desk with the mouse. I even set up the iPad.

And wouldn't you know it, things went smoothly.

With one presentation left, I was nearly in the clear. The last student made her way to the front of the room. The high school principal, who had popped in to observe, smiled approvingly. A few students yawned. And then, without warning, the door to the classroom opened and in walked the superintendent. Of course.

The students stopped yawning and postures improved as he strode to the back of the room and pulled out a chair.

With a deep breath, I pressed "record" on the iPad, pulled out a rubric, and...everything froze.

"This has never happened before," I said. On the screen, that harbinger of doom appeared: the spinning rainbow wheel. "Oh, it's frozen, this has never happened before," I repeated dumbly.

"Force the shutdown!" called the superintendent from the back. I stared blankly at the computer. The wheel spun on and on. I closed my eyes and wished I was back in Egypt.
The principal stood up and joined me.
"Force the shutdown," he repeated.
"I don't know how," I whispered awkwardly.

My students came to the rescue, shouting random combinations over each other. As the computer finally shut down, I risked a glance at the superintendent, expecting the worst.

He looked back at me. Then he shrugged. That was it. Here I was, sprouting grey hairs over a frozen computer, and his response seemed to say, "Eh, it happens." My response to that was visible relief. I know it was visible because the iPad recorded the entire thing so I could relive the moment over and over.

One day, perhaps in the near future, I'll be a technophile myself. I'll know how to handle the spinning pinwheel. I will stop thinking of tablets as "Thou shalt not kill" and start associating them with "Allow push notifications?" I will take you outside and point at the sky and say with confidence, "My files are somewhere up there. I understand this."

For now, I am content to learn from my students, even if it means admitting that I have no idea what a fiber optic is. And if the fate of the free world rests on someone opening a combination locker or correctly identifying Moby in a photograph, I will gladly make myself useful.

*Nicole Gough hails from Middletown, New Jersey. You may remember her from such stories as "Raw Meat and Mixed Metaphors."*

# THE GOOD SAMARITAN, CHINESE-STYLE

## Kathryn Turner

"Why don't we go somewhere *you* haven't been?"

It was early January. Mom had been with us in Guangzhou for two weeks. She was 85, but she looked and moved like a woman at least 10 years younger. She and my dad had done lots of foreign travel; she was always up for a new adventure. She'd flown to China to be with us for Christmas and we'd already done the standard Guangzhou sights. We'd strolled the peaceful tree-lined streets of Shamian Island, the small space designated as Guangzhou's foreign enclave in the 1800s. We'd braved the famous Qing Ping Market, full of exotic ingredients for traditional Chinese medicine such as tree fungi as large as dinner plates, open sacks of tortoise shells, and dead lizards flayed on sticks. We'd toured the Temple of the Nanyue King, an archaeological site discovered in the 1980s at a construction site, and we had sampled some of China's huge variety of cuisine at neighborhood restaurants.

Mom and I sat together in our 25th floor apartment looking at a brochure that one of my colleagues had given me just that week. It was about an ancestral Qing Dynasty home and gardens built in the mid-1800s called Yu Yin Shan Fang. This colleague had recently toured it and thought it well worth a visit. She told me how easy it would be to get to, and said, "You can take the new subway line. The stop's at the end of the line." Although I'd lived in Guangzhou for only a few months, I knew the subway system pretty well. It was streamlined, efficient, and easy to use. Using the metro to get to this new place was appealing. Mom especially liked the excursion idea because it would be a new experience for me, not just her.

That weekend, Mom and I left our apartment early in the afternoon and walked to the nearest subway station. I studied the map to learn how to get to line 4, memorizing the name of the last station. We boarded the first train and were on our way. Line 4, being so new, had only a few passengers. Many of our fellow car-mates looked newly arrived from the countryside and stared openly at us throughout the ride. I was a little surprised that it took around an hour to get to the last stop, later learning that my colleague hadn't herself taken the subway but instead had hired a car to get there and back. The buildings outside the subway stop were low and nondescript. The sidewalks had only a few pedestrians, unlike Guangzhou's perpetually-filled ones. I was surprised again that the taxi ride from the station was fairly long. Never mind—we still had plenty of time to tour the estate. The taxi driver dropped us at the front gate, we got our tickets, and began our exploration.

There were very few other visitors at Yu Yin Shan Fang. The ancestral home felt almost too quiet—like we'd discovered an abandoned property. Inside the estate's gates were covered corridors, pavilions, small man-made lotus ponds, some with arched bridges, and the occasional piece of antique-looking furniture. In one of the pavilions we happened upon a group of musicians playing Chinese classical instruments, so we sat and listened to the concert with its distinctive twangs, feeling lucky to experience a little extra bonus on our tour.

When we decided that we'd seen about all of Yu Yin, we found the exit to grab a taxi back to the subway stop. By now it was early evening, but there was still plenty of light. The street was unexpectedly empty—the few shops there were already shuttered. "Let's walk down the road and see if we can get to a busier street," I suggested to Mom. There were no sidewalks but walking in the street posed no danger—not only were there no taxis, there were no cars or trucks at all. A man on a motorcycle rode by, making broad gestures to us and pointing to the seat behind him. "No thanks," I gestured back. More walking. Still no taxis; only Motorcycle Man driving back and forth, trying his best to sell us on a ride with him. *No way*, I thought, *will I subject my 85-year-old mother to riding on a motorcycle!*

Finally, after another fifteen minutes or so of walking, we arrived at a small but not particularly charming town plaza. I searched to no avail for a taxi stand. There were no taxis at all. As I gazed around, wondering what our next step should be, a small crowd formed, encircling us. Having been in southern China only five months, my Mandarin and Cantonese were nearly nonexistent. I gamely tried to convey our need to get back to Guangzhou. The responses were some bemused looks and even laughter, but nothing else was forthcoming. After more time standing around with no help in the offing, a few police officers joined our group. *Ah, this could be promising*, I thought. But I had to shake my head and shrug my shoulders at their questions in Chinese, and just kept repeating "Guangzhou—taxi—subway." The officers left as soon as it was apparent that communication with us would be futile.

Dusk was fast approaching and with it, a chill in the air. I looked around the square in despair. Would Mom and I have to spend the night in some fleabag hotel? How much cash did I have with me? Not very much, I realized. I looked at Mom, who seemed not the least bit perturbed; she and our onlookers just kept smiling and laughing at one another. She pointed to some interesting features in different women's clothing, nodding her approval. *Breathe*, I told myself, *Mom is certainly enjoying herself.* I hadn't yet joined the ranks of cell phone users nor did I know anyone's telephone number back in Guangzhou, so phoning home was not an option.

Suddenly, the crowd looked toward a young man, tall and thin, striding quickly across the square in our direction. The crowd began gesticulating and grew louder, more animated. He stopped in front of Mom and me and asked, "I help you?" I told him we needed to get back to Guangzhou. There ensued some discussion between him and our little throng, which allowed me a few moments to look him over. He was wearing a short-sleeved white button-down shirt—a little frayed at the collar—and carried a lightweight polyester black suit jacket over his arm. He had a studious quality about him, especially with his dark-rimmed glasses. I pegged him to be in his twenties. He looked around thoughtfully and then gestured to us to follow him.

Without any hesitation, I took Mom's hand and we hurried along behind him to a small bus nearby, awkwardly smiling as he continued to beckon us along. The three of us got on, and soon the bus was on its way. "You from where come?" he asked, "Meiguo?" "No," I replied, "USA." He looked perplexed. I learned later that Meiguo is Mandarin for America. We gamely tried more conversation. "You stay in Guangzhou?" "Well, I live there—not just visiting." More awkward nodding and smiling once our conversational gambits were exhausted. We took the little bus for a short ride to a street where several large buses were parked. He ushered us onto one of them and found two seats for Mom and me at the front. He found himself a spot several rows back and sat in silence throughout the ride. I felt dazed at the predicament we'd been in, and the quick turn of events with the help of this young man.

The ride was long, more than an hour, and it was dark when we got back to the city. Our young man began looking more closely at the streets we passed, finally standing up as the bus turned a corner, motioning us to follow him to the back exit. As if by magic, the moment we were off the bus and it had pulled away, a taxi drove up in its place. "You stay in Guangzhou?" I asked. He shook his head and said, "I return to village." He glanced at his watch, suit jacket still draped on his arm, peering around the intersection as Mom and I got in the waiting cab. Through the window, I was only able to offer a quick thank you—"xie xie"— to our Good Samaritan before the taxi sped off to bring us through familiar streets and back to our apartment building. Mom chatted excitedly about the day. When I mentioned to her my anxiety about getting back, she told me she'd had complete trust in me. *Really*, I thought to myself, *her trust should have been in our young man.* And I never even learned his name.

*Kathryn Turner, who grew up in a Chicago suburb, worked in a variety of of libraries during her 36-year career as a librarian: university, corporate, public, and school. She worked for 14 years in the US and 22 years abroad in Pakistan, Cote d'Ivoire, Venezuela, China, and the Dominican Republic. She also served as a Peace Corps volunteer in the Congo (Zaire) for two years. She is now happily retired and living in Florida.*

# WHITE NOISE
*Carmel Pezzullo*

White noise. I had heard of the phenomenon of white noise but never really experienced it personally. White noise is the idea that all things happening are drowned out, allowing you to focus all of your energy on one task only. White noise was the only reason I was able to get myself out of that bus, to find that one possible exit. To block the screams, to mask the smell of blood, to hold back the tears, to resist the fear—and to realise that it would take some time for my life to ever really be the same again.

I had been living and teaching in Colombia for two years when I decided to spend a summer travelling through Chile and Bolivia. I was coming to the end of my six-week trip and had just spent four days in the highest capital city in the world, La Paz, before exploring the islands of Lake Titicaca.

It's the day of my departure, the bus passes by my hostel soon after 8:00 a.m.; I get on and settle into seat number four, near the window. We drive around La Paz for about an hour, picking up the other passengers, until we pull in unexpectedly to the bus terminal. As soon as the doors hiss open, a crowd moves, pushes, and shoves its way onto the bus, filling it up. Amongst the chaos, a Japanese couple, speaking no English or Spanish, gesture to me that I am in one of their seats. I notice their small ticket indicating that seats four and five are theirs. I smile gently. All the seats are now occupied, and the aisle is still full of people. I spot a woman with a clipboard, a good sign—she can help sort out this mess.

It seems the clipboard lady has an itemised list of seat numbers with corresponding names. I give her my name and ask for my seat number. She declares that my name is not on the list and that I am to get off. I insist that I have already paid and that I am on the right bus. I ask her to check again, and after four attempts we both realise that my name has been spelt incorrectly, and that seat eleven is my assigned seat. There have been four attempts to get me off this bus, four chances I have to find another way to the islands, but my ordered and organised upbringing prevails: I know I have paid and am supposed to be a passenger on this bus. To my amazement, seat eleven is empty, and I shuffle over, put the armrest down, and settle in for the long ride. Little do I know that this small decision, to lower my armrest, is to be my most important decision.

We drive for two hours. I notice that we are starting to descend. We are moving pretty fast at times, and as we enter another steep descent, it feels as though we are speeding downhill. What happens next takes only a few seconds. The bus becomes very unstable and begins swinging dangerously from side to side as its wheels lift off the ground. I can feel my body rising from the seat. It is evident that the bus driver is losing control as he attempts to navigate small curves in the windy road. People begin to scream. I try to maintain composure and think we'll be fine, but then we aren't. The bus makes a sudden lurch and the driver completely loses control...it rolls left with so much force that we become airborne. We flip completely over in the air and come crashing down, very heavily, on the left side of the bus, shattering all the left side windows. The noise is deafening.

Over the next few seconds my eyes dart around as I try to take in the reality of what has just happened. I see tangled bodies, I hear moaning and high-pitched screaming, and can smell a mixture of blood and dust. No seatbelts on the bus means that during the impact, people have been thrown around like crash dummies.

After a few moments, I realise that I have not fallen down to the left side of the bus, but that I am in fact hunched over something and suspended above. That simple decision to put my armrest down has meant that as the bus landed on its side, the armrest caught me and minimized the impact.

I try to stand up. One hand reaches up and grabs the baggage shelf above my head as the other lifts the armrest. I find it hard to block out the screaming and chaos around me. I try lifting somebody off another person, but they just squeal in pain. I try to move some bags to clear space for people and discover that everything I touch is splattered red. As I look around, I notice the Japanese couple in seats four and five. The woman, in the window seat, has her eyes closed, and her partner, holding his arm in pain, is trying to coax her back to consciousness. This is the first time I almost lose composure. *That could have been me*, I think to myself, *in seat four.*

The only exit, at the front of the bus, is now blocked. I know the only real way to help is to find another way out. Whilst most of the passengers are injured and panicking, I look up at the windows, usually on the right side of the bus, now above me. Those windows are our only escape.

Realising I am too short, I ask a taller man to help me open the window above. He tries but to no avail. I beg him to try again, but he looks at me with hopeless eyes. It's up to me. As I try to jump up, I discover to my horror that I am standing on another person. Things are escalating quickly. I move over, leap high, and try to open another window. It too is stuck.

White noise.

This window is all I can see, all I can focus on. I have to get it open, get out, and find help. I try again and punch the handle to help it slide open. I do this many times before it finally moves, but just an inch.

White noise.

With all my strength, I jump up and push, jump up and push until it opens. And now to get out. Upper body strength was never my forte; I have never yet been able to complete a full chin-up.

White noise.

With all my might I leap again, grab the frame, pull myself all the way up, and squeeze my way out.

Even though we are somewhere in the mountains with nothing but trees in sight, a group of locals have heard the crash and are running to help. The next six hours, in blood-stained clothing, is a mixture of translating and helping where I can. Getting to the closest hospital, back in La Paz, proves to be our biggest challenge.

I'm still not sure why but I walk away injury-free, without so much as even a scratch.

I spent the next few years dealing with the lingering trauma from that day. I refused to believe that the accident had affected me in any way. Admitting that aspects of travel scared me was hard to handle. But with professional help and the powerful guidance, acceptance, and love of my dear teaching friends, I've slowly been able to desensitise many of the accident's effects on me, even though it still is difficult to ride on windy roads.

I may still have fears based on that experience, but they don't define me. In fact, my travel has become more ambitious than ever: crossing the tumultuous Drake Passage to visit Antarctica, soaring above the temples of Myanmar in a hot air balloon, and four-wheeling through the sand dunes of Northern Brazil.

White noise is the idea that all things happening are drowned out, allowing you to focus all of your energy on one task only. White noise was the only reason I was able to get myself out of that bus, to find that one possible exit.

And the white noise, as frightening as it was, gave me clarity, a more direct understanding of what I believe, what I value, and who I am. Fear shouldn't limit anyone. Each moment is not guaranteed. Travel is a part of my identity.

*Carmel Pezzullo, a native of Melbourne, Australia, teaches in Hong Kong. She has taught in elementary schools for 12 years, 2 in Australia and 10 in Spain, Colombia, China, and Hong Kong.*

# THE FIRST WEEK IN BANGKOK CAN MAKE A GROWN MAN WEEP
## *Jalal Tarazi*

So, there we were, standing on the side of Sukhumvit Road (the major street through eastern Bangkok) under the BTS skytrain station, sweating from the humidity, standing knee-deep in rainwater, jet-lagged, sucking in the nasty fumes of the many decades-old Bangkok buses, and trying to hail a taxi. After two years teaching in Bahrain and four in Maui, I thought the transition to my new teaching job would be easy. I couldn't have been more wrong. If the first week in Bahrain was like the comforting shoulder of a best friend, and the first week in Hawaii was like being welcomed to a five-star beach resort, then the first week in Bangkok was like getting mugged by a meth addict. It was arduous and tiring on a level that I can't even begin to describe.

On the first day, our time being escorted around central Bangkok by a returning teacher was problem-free, but it was the time four of us new teachers spent trying to get back to the hotel that was, without a doubt, the worst hour I have ever spent in any city.

Bangkok has an above-ground electric train called the Bangkok Transit System (BTS). At the time, the terminal stop in the eastern end of the city was On Nut station, and our hotel was located an additional fifteen minutes away from this stop. On Nut is typically very busy, but there are so many taxis available that one rarely needs to wait longer than five minutes—unless, that is, it is pissing down rain as it was the day I arrived in Bangkok. In the tropics during the rainy season, enough rain can fall within one hour that the streets turn into a fast-moving flood plain. With Bangkok at sea level, the canals and storm drains get so inundated that water is actually forced back up to the streets. Although I have yet to see this, I have heard several stories of ten-foot-long pythons being pushed up into the streets from the flood drains. You can just imagine how difficult it is finding a taxi during this type of deluge.

We spent more than half an hour trying to find a taxi, our umbrellas no match for the rainstorms that enveloped us. I wanted to cry. Honking horns, curtains of water, and no solution in sight. The weepy voice in my head kept saying, "What am I doing here? I left the beautiful beaches and mountains in Maui for this?!"

Finally we hustled into a taxi, about as much water coming in with us as I had used in my last shower back in the US. When I told the driver where we wanted to go, I said the name—Avana Hotel—as an American would pronounce it, placing emphasis on the second syllable, "aVAna." The taxi driver's response of "Hmmm?" encouraged me to repeat myself.

"aVAna."
"Hmmm?"

This went on for almost a minute. As I contemplated giving up, opening the door, and rolling out into the street river, one of the new teachers remembered that she had the hotel card in her pocket. When she passed it to the driver, he said, "Ahhhh, avaNA!" For some reason, whenever Thais who don't speak English say an English word, they always, and I do mean always, put the emphasis on the last syllable. Add to this the fact that only eight consonant sounds in the Thai language end a word, you get some interesting interpretations of English. The "R" sound cannot be a final consonant sound, so comPUter becomes compuTEH, nor can the "L" sound be a final consonant sound, so NOOdle becomes nooDEN. My name Jalal becomes Jalan or Jalau, depending on who I am talking to. Fighting through the standstill traffic (but, thankfully, no ten-foot long pythons), we made it to the hotel but our stress was far from over.

Unlike Bahrain, where the school gave me my settling-in allowance in cash when they dropped me off at my fully-furnished apartment, my new school had us first open a bank account, after which they immediately deposited the money. This didn't happen until a few days after we arrived in Bangkok, and since many apartments wanted rent for the first and last months along with a security deposit, our "settling-in allowance" was desperately needed for things other than what would help us settle in.

Over the next week-and-a-half, many of us had to find an apartment while also going through our orientation at school. We walked around the city after school and during the weekend, looking for possible places, but could not find one that worked with the right space, location, and configuration. Finding an apartment on my own was difficult enough, but with most of the small street signs only in Thai, I had no idea where I was nor how to get back to any apartment. Even if I could remember a street name, what were the odds that the taxi driver would understand me when I wanted to go back in the following days?

I tried to triangulate myself with a 7-11 or some place similar, but 7-11s are on every street corner in Bangkok. Funny that a dose of "home" was keeping me from finding a new one.

I had been living out of my suitcase for about five nights, tired of losing my toothbrush, searching for clean underwear, and futilely attempting to get rid of the crick in my neck from not having my own comfortable pillow. I was ready to settle on any place just to avoid a meltdown.

Desperate, I lassoed a taxi driver to take me to one final recommended place. As we zipped through back alleys and crossed small canals left and right, I had no idea where I was. I might as well have been blindfolded. Suddenly we turned into a large apartment building with a pool, nice views, and a close proximity to the BTS. And of course, there was a 7-11 right down the street! The agent showed me only one room but I had seen enough. I was practically signing the paperwork as he was showing me how the shower worked. I didn't care if I couldn't tell a taxi how to get back here. I had just surrendered to Bangkok.

I ended up living in that apartment for six years and am now in my twelfth year living in Thailand. Although it took some time, Bangkok and Thailand became as comforting as the shoulder of a best friend and as welcoming as a five-star resort. I just needed to weather the initial storm to find out I would eventually call this place home.

*Jalal Tarazi, was born in Beirut, Lebanon but raised in Connecticut, USA. He has taught high school science for 22 years. He taught in Connecticut for two years before attending his first international job fair conference. Since then he has worked in Bahrain, Hawaii, Bangkok, and is currently working in Phuket, Thailand.*

# SOME NOTES ON GRACE
*Jess Barga*

I grew up in Ohio with schoolteacher parents. Before 2012, my knowledge of nannies sounded like "A Spoonful of Sugar" with a little "Lonely Goatherd" mixed in. Mary Poppins and Maria may as well have been hobbits or elves for all the real-world relevance they had in my life. If you had told me before I moved abroad that when I had a child of my own, my husband and I would raise him with the full-time help of a paid employee, I would have scoffed. It's not just that hiring a nanny in the US can break the bank—on top of the extravagance, for me there was a sense of *wrongdoing* about it, surely a side effect of my middle-class upbringing. Have a kid? Well, then, raise the kid. Do the heavy lifting yourself. Of course, that was before I learned that in the world of parenting, I'm a total lightweight.

When Cormac was born we were teaching in Venezuela. A month of cooking, cleaning, and child-rearing services cost about $150. Neither of us had any desire to give up our jobs for more than a few months, even if our school would have let us. Any misgivings we had about hiring a nanny dissolved, and when we moved to China three years later, it was assumed with no discussion that we'd have full-time domestic help. It's amazing how quickly your values shift in the face of a happy kid and a fridge full of healthy, home-cooked food, especially when you've already given yourself over to the voluntary helplessness that international schools allow their teachers to foster. Sometimes it really does feel like we're in a sort of assisted living situation.

Cormac's nannies haven't been just a source of babysitting and sustenance, though. They've been an education for us all, by far our most valuable insight to the cultures we've perched on the fringes of for years. First with Celia in Caracas and now with Ching-ah in Guangzhou, we've come to regard these women as trusted and beloved family members, and the sentiment feels mutual. It's true, of course, that you don't pay your family, and in both places we've had more seasoned colleagues warn us of the folly of regarding your hired caregiver as a friend or a loved one. But in the end, emotion has trumped economics: we've disregarded the advice flagrantly, and have never looked back.

We stumbled on Celia, a young grandmother who had raised five children of her own, through a friend of a friend, with no clear reference trail and little more than intuition to guide us. The process of interviewing and proposing a salary made me nervous, but Celia is a woman who casts aside your discomfort with her first smile and a single utterance of *Ay, mi amor*. She knew children and babies vastly better than I ever will. Not only was she accomplished at child-rearing, but her experience teaching her own daughters to care for their babies was ample, and it's no exaggeration to say that she taught me—no, both Chris and me—how to be parents. I hope I'm right in saying that to this day we raise Cormac with her blend of affection and firmness, character formation and fun.

Beyond the obvious and expected lessons, though, Celia opened my eyes to the reality of life as a working-class Latina in a country still struggling (and currently, not even trying) to create opportunities for all of its people. She told stories. Some were joyful and nostalgic, scenes from her children's younger days or tales of a simpler life in lovely rural Venezuela. But others left me speechless.

The story I remember best came on an afternoon when I returned from school, shaken by a conversation with the woman who cleaned my classroom about the vicious dispute she was enduring with her feckless ex-husband. This *sinvergüenza* had abandoned her for a sixteen-year-old as soon as she became pregnant with their third child. I told Celia about it, wondering what my friend could possibly do. Celia's face, normally a picture of warmth, took on a grim cast. She said, "This is how life is in this place. That man will never listen to words."

Celia went on to tell me about her own husband in their younger days, his heavy drinking, and all the predictable abuses that accompanied it. One evening, after a lavish bender, he came home hours late and demanded dinner. When she put it in front of him and it wasn't what he wanted, he grew furious, shoving all the food and then Celia to the ground and kicking her, then passing out on the bed in their tiny home. "Jessie," she told me, staring at me with steely eyes that shone with tears, "I waited until José was snoring. Then I picked up the frying pan I made that dinner in. I brought it down on his legs with all my might, three, four times. José didn't walk for two weeks. He never complained. And he hasn't raised a hand against me since." I believed her: I'd met him; Cormac knew him well. Celia's husband, now a quiet and kindly 60-something, seemed devoted and affectionate.

When we moved to Guangzhou, China in 2015, we fell into a situation as enviable as ours in Venezuela had been. Ching-ah, our second nanny, is not just good-hearted but, well, *best-*

hearted, quite likely the most caring and selfless person I've ever known. Her bond with Cormac seemed firm almost from day one, and now, after three years together, she and I frequently sign text messages with "I love you" and tear up when we greet each other at the end of a holiday. A superwoman among *ayis* (literally 'auntie', this Mandarin word encompasses everything from cleaning staff to actual blood relations), she cares for Cormac before and after school, keeps our house immaculately clean, cooks multiple dishes every day, and also cooks and cleans for two of our colleagues while Cormac is at school. Among the small, fortunate group of teachers who employ Ching-ah, we like to joke about her abundant apologies. When she cooks an incredible dinner, she's sorry she used up the tomatoes. If she takes Cormac to the park, she's sorry he got sweaty. When we take her out for a thank-you dinner at the end of every school year, she's *very* sorry that she didn't just make us all a multi-course meal instead. This endearing quirk is genuinely representative of Ching-ah's identity: she is full of love—not doing all she can to help feels unnatural and uncomfortable to her.

One rainy winter night, Ching-Ah was blindsided by a motorized bicycle, unregulated hazards that cruise the sidewalks here soundlessly and swiftly. She was taken to the hospital, unconscious with a concussion, but returned to work only two days later (feeling, as you'd expect, more sorry than ever for not discharging her duties adequately). Mortified, we doted on her, reminding her several times a day that she should rest and refrain from doing any serious work at our house. Our reminders were too frequent, it turned out: she tired quickly of the special treatment, and found a way to dispense with it. As I urged her a few days later to stop cleaning, she turned and looked at me with measured calm. In a patchwork of English, gestures, and the little Chinese she knew I understood, she put things in perspective for me: "My children were both breach. On the nights that they were born, my husband was out with his friends drinking. They were born at home, with only my mother to help. *This is not a big deal.*" My eyes widened; I nodded. I kept my mouth closed. Point taken.

Sometimes I wonder what we must look like to these valiant, wise, benevolent women. They observe our strange, foreign ways—the fact that we spend $25 a week on sparkling water but refuse to eat their expertly seasoned beef; or that Chris, in spite of his Y chromosome, does his own dishes and happily stays home with Cormac while I close down the bars—without comment. Although we may mystify each other at times, the human warmth and connection between us is palpable. We share the same basic motivations, the same love of our children, and the desire for a peaceful life where we're free to make our own choices and do more meaningful things than just work and survive. Their first-hand accounts of life as women of the working class, though, and the fact that these ordeals don't dent their deep wells of compassion and devotion are what make me look at women like Celia and Ching-ah with an admiration verging on awe.

It's not as though we don't think about privilege on a daily basis, we first-world foreigners, interlopers in countries where, directly or indirectly, the exploitation of the poor and vulnerable has been conducted for centuries by rich countries like the ones we're from or, as in China, by a seemingly omnipotent elite. Of course we think about it, and wonder whether our work there is, on a small scale, somehow symbolic of that exploitation. But how often do we stare it in the face? The expat bubble, you know, gets quite opaque if you allow it to, and most of us do let it, at least when we're wrapped up in our own stress and drama. I'm as guilty as the next foreigner of embracing the exotic cuisine and ignoring the real lives of people on the street. But the people in your home and heart are not the people on the street. Celia and Ching-ah are fighting in their own ways to be treated as fully human in places where their class and gender don't automatically confer that right. They're doing so in a way that reminds the observer that their humanity is, perhaps, more complex and profound than our own. The least we can do is pause and acknowledge what they're doing, and take a few notes on what grace actually looks like.

*Jess Barga was born in Cincinnati, OH, and teaches in Guangzhou, China. She's been teaching high school English and Spanish for 17 years: 5 in Seattle, WA; 12 in South Korea, Venezuela, and China.*

# JUST EAST OF THE NEW WEST
## *Chris Pultz*

It was a Friday night in Minsk, about a month into a two-year teaching contract, and while most of my colleagues were taking the train to Vilnius, I was staying behind getting ready for a date.

There'd been a lot of talk of Lithuania's capital city since I'd arrived a month earlier. To some, it was a model for what a post-socialist capital should be: a city whose squares and narrow walkways are interchangeable with those found in Western Europe, a city with English films and friendly, English-speaking people. To my Belarusian colleagues, the feeling was unilateral: Vilnius had shopping. It was the new West, just a two-and-a-half-hour drive away, accessible only with a visa.

Unlike Vilnius, Minsk was not spared by the Great Patriotic War. Minsk did not have those charming narrow walkways, nor did it have great shopping. Instead it had runway-wide boulevards good for landing Russian TU-95s in a pinch, monoliths with red stars perched above, and social realism, an architectural style that ranged from the stately and imposing to the functional and drafty. Western films were dubbed in Russian, and it was difficult to find an English speaker. This made life harder for both tourists and expatriates, but it also made it arguably more authentic, and rather than spend my weekend in a place that was relatively more comfortable, I wanted to make things work here. And so it was with a more-than-temperate pride that I carried myself onto a crowded trolleybus headed to meet two young Belarusian ladies in the city center.

I'd met the girls the previous Sunday. It had been a long afternoon grading papers in my apartment, so I decided to venture out for a change in scenery. I sought out the lone Irish pub, but was initially put off by the "reserved" signs not just on the tables but on the horseshoe-shaped bar itself. I learned soon enough that the signs were more of a "right to refuse." There was always room for the desired few. Halfway through my first Guinness, I noticed the girls; one of them kept looking across the bar. She had thick, curly brown hair and a tight smile that underscored pale blue eyes.

Sopping up some courage from my second beer, and growing tired of careting-in missing articles and prepositions, I ventured over, only to find that neither spoke English. With a helpless smile, it was now my turn to face the grammatical music. Through my Russian phrasebook and some shredded German, we managed. The more outgoing of the two was Anna; Nastya was her friend with the smile and the eyes. We traded numbers and agreed to meet the following Friday, when they said they'd show me around and help me with my Russian.

I arrived at the city center early, and after taking in the gold-onion dome of the Orthodox cathedral kitty-corner from a bas-relief war memorial, I decided to cross back in time over the Svislach River, venturing into the sliver of old city spared by the

Nazis. For my friends back in New York who knew Minsk as more than a passing reference from the sitcom "Friends," and those whose grandparents had survived the war and had lived here, this neighborhood was just as they would remember: painted stucco facades and picture windows, red-tiled roofs, and narrow, cobbled streets made for strolling on Sunday afternoons.

Not wanting to be late, I walked back towards the trolleybus station and saw two familiar faces. We exchanged pleasantries in Russian; that was as far as my language skills could take me. We walked, Anna on one side, Nastya on the other. Anna took my phrasebook from me while Nastya broke the spine of a basic Russian grammar book. She must have just bought it. That was encouraging.

I tried to slip in some English, but they kept on in Russian, as any good teacher would.

We moved back towards the old city. It seemed it was a favorite of theirs as well. Passing cars, shrubs, and staircases: each became language lessons. Anna would turn and point, "Ma-shi-na."

"Ma-shi-na," I'd repeat. Minutes later, pointing to a car, she'd see if I remembered.

This game continued as we walked towards the opera house. The spectacle attracted the curious look and occasional smile of passersby. The night had been my best yet in Minsk. I wasn't grading papers or stuck in my apartment or wandering the city on my own, stopping only to point at pictures in a menu. Dusk had settled in, and it was still warm. There'd be many cold nights to come hunkered in my apartment, and I wasn't ready to get back on the trolleybus.

I pulled out a language exercise book, and Anna grabbed it. Nastya sat beside her, and they walked me through my current lesson on direction words and gendered possessive pronouns. "There her boyfriend. There his girlfriend," they said pointing to passing couples, the man often—in an act of Slavic chivalry— holding his girlfriend's purse. Russian was tough in its own ways: deciphering Cyrillic and reaching for the correct noun endings pressed me to the point of embolism, but it had no present form of being, no abstraction concerning life in the present. There was simply a subject and its modifiers.

We continued until my brain spasmed. I suggested a bit of English.
"Okay," said Nastya.
Anna was quiet.
"Why you here?" Nastya asked.
"Existentially?" I joked. "Okay, sorry. Why am I here in Minsk?"
"Yes," she said, smiling and nodding.
Anna shuffled a bit.

I explained slowly and as best I could, because I really didn't know.

I said something about loving to travel, that I'd taught abroad in several different places, and that it excited me to see how different people lived; I even said something stupid about liking to try the local food and drink. It sounded hollow, but how could I get into the deeper stuff? In the episodic life of an international teacher, a life carved in each new place ventured, was I willing to admit, even to myself, that with each move I get to start again?

A few ample droplets from above forced us to close the books, and we sought cover in the trolleybus station. Anna was growing sullen.
"You like German?" I asked.
"Yes," said Anna.

"You go to Germany?"

"No."

"Um," said Nastya. She squinted, trying to will the word to her tongue. Flipping through her book, "Ya, okay, I know this word. Visa, no visa."

I looked back at Anna. She spoke the language fluently, worked for a German company, took Irish step-dancing classes, yet couldn't venture west of the Belarusian border. Without sponsorship or a husband, without opening herself to the kind of scrutiny a Westerner couldn't conceive of, without being able to offer financial "proof" that she'd return, there couldn't even be a shopping trip in Vilnius.

I should have stuck to the pronouns.

We said our goodbyes as I boarded the whiny trolleybus, doors creaking shut in front of me and my slowly waving arm. The bus passed through the wooded area, opening for one quick look at the opera house's erupting fountain before being replaced by storefronts and block houses.

With the rain still at a drizzle, I skipped the transfer and decided instead to walk the long stretch of boulevard towards my apartment. An assortment of pedestrians passed opposite me: women in heels, a group of soldiers, a ruddy-faced drunk, a pack of teens on skateboards. I smelled the McDonalds before I saw it, the drive-thru line snaking out into the road, the inside equally packed for a taste of Westernization.

Continuing on past a construction site, I heard a mewing up ahead somewhere within the fenced-off mounds of dirt. It sounded like a kitten. I continued on in the direction of its rapid cries. Couples and friends walked past, even young children seeming deaf to the noise. Crouching along the foot of the fence, I saw its marbled grey coat. Staring up at me, it began to parade itself in front of its background of gravel, rubbing its side along the rusted chain-link fence.

I reached my fingers through an opening to pet it, but it recoiled just out of reach. It continued mewing. "What do you want?" I said.

It looked away but continued its cry. Perhaps it was asking me the same.

I stood up and walked on as the mewing persisted, but it was soon drowned out by the trolley buses' whines. I continued along the broad boulevard of a place I had never dreamed of living, a place I would soon grow fond of, yet a place I was always free to leave.

*Chris Pultz, a native of Long Island, New York, teaches in Istanbul, Turkey. He has taught middle and high school English for 19 years, 7 in the US and 12 in Madagascar, Hungary, Belarus, and Turkey.*

# RECOGNIZING THE SIGNALS
*Yvonne Ricketts*

"Can you believe we are here?" I asked my husband as we sipped the frothy ale served in humongous, punchbowl-esque steins at a quaint beer garden steps from our new home in Vilnius, Lithuania. Our eyes took in the rich diversity of European architecture, the narrow cobblestone streets, and hot air balloons floating through the blue skies. It felt like we were on a Disneyland ride for adults.

That August, while settling into our new life chapter, the thrill of being abroad again made for a honeymoon like no other. The glorious long summer days, the discovery of a new place, and all our newcomer misadventures were celebrated with excellent brew shared amongst new friends. The view of the Old Town from our school was breathtaking, including the ancient castle. That view made up for the small classrooms and narrow hallways in our very old Russian-style facility, originally built only for kindergarteners but now serving K-12 students. The hot summer days quickly turned to cold ones in early September, taking us by surprise. "What do you mean we won't have heat until the city determines it is cold enough to be turned on?"

We were told to "be brave" for an indefinite time after the water was turned off in our building. However, the walk to school among the vibrant autumn trees erased any ill will.

I look back and think of the work it took for my husband and me to secure overseas positions in our mid-fifties—the gratitude we felt, not only that we could afford to do this, but also that our grown children were successfully independent. We were elated to be able to work in a part of Europe where travel was easy and affordable. We both felt we could push aside the stateside family concerns for aging parents, leaving siblings to deal with the necessary care, and we assumed our children could carry on and live their lives, connecting with us when possible. We relished the international school and expat culture that we had experienced ten years earlier, remembering the adventures but not the stresses, the opportunities but not the challenges.

The first hint that we were missing home was when, visiting Paris for the first time, we were notified of the death of a dear friend. Our time walking the streets was marked with joy and sorrow. We felt our friend's presence at a bread shop that carried his name. We bought lots of rich, buttery Parisian bread but ate it in silence while wandering slowly in the Tuileries. We felt the pain of our loss as we lit candles in the darkened, quiet sanctuaries of the Notre Dame Cathedral and Sacre Coeur Basilica. And we sharpened our determination to live each day more fully as we toasted him with champagne high in the Eiffel Tower. "Do you think we should go home?" I asked my husband as we contemplated how hard it was to be so far away at at a time like this, unable to comfort and help loved ones. The guilt we both felt at being in Paris while those at home were suffering bubbled to the surface, only to be washed away by another outstanding museum or dinner before the strong tide of guilt came back again.

Despite the experience in Paris, we remained abroad and thrived in many ways. We celebrated our ability to host our children for three consecutive years of Christmas holidays in dreamlike venues in France, Portugal, Spain, and Italy. It felt like we had won the lottery, to be able to laugh and eat our way through these places with our children. We stayed at quaint crowded Airbnbs or lavish hotels with views, ate too much rich food, were awed by fascinating museums, reveled in the history, tried grappa and absinthe, and enjoyed the luxury of it all. Such wonderful memories tempered the aches of homesickness. But those aches were real and intense.

When our niece was planning her wedding and inquired about possible dates we could attend, and we realized there was not even one that would work, we felt defeated by our choice to live abroad. The living-abroad-balloon was losing air. The challenge of important connections with family became increasingly acute. Our son became engaged, and the wedding preparations being made at home often could not include us. A tragic accident involving a sibling, and the long-term impact on her life, was not only a shock, but an unpleasant and frustrating reality.

When we did go back to the US for visits, we shared joyful meals and caught up with family in my aging mother-in-law's welcoming beach house in California. But these feel-good moments were displaced by the sadness in her eyes each time we departed. Equally compelling was our own lovely stateside home by the sea, tempting us with the possibilities of a retired lifestyle at home near family. As we gazed at the beautiful view of the bay, we would often ask ourselves, "Did we make the right decision to go back overseas?"

At the same time, our positions at school did not provide us with the job satisfaction we had imagined. The country was also changing—visa requirements for expats became more difficult, and the government had new crises to deal with. The threat of Russian invasion was ever present, always talked about by locals and diplomats in hallways and at parties. We continued to tick off many cities on our European bucket list, yet at the end of our third year abroad, we felt ready to go home, exhausted from both the job and traveling while feeling the need to share family responsibilities.

But when the opportunity to work at another international school in another country presented itself, we took it like bait off a hook—readily and with blinding optimism that all would be well. We would finally learn Spanish! We would explore South America! Not long after arriving in Argentina, we realized that the signals to return home didn't disappear, they were flashing even brighter. Our two years there found us back home in California for almost every school break. Our resolve to live abroad, away from family and friends, was weakening. Also, significant changes were happening in the US. I became interested in doing more than just working and traveling: to be an active—not passive—social justice participant in my native country. I felt helpless living in Argentina, at the bottom of the world, watching the rights I took for granted start to erode. I felt motivated to do something and knew, for me, that meant a return home.

My mother in-law's death was by far the most anguishing experience of our time in Argentina. The fast decline of her health, her visible despair at not being able to speak to us via FaceTime, the uncertainty of when to return home for her final days, and the inability to provide physical support for siblings were agonizing to deal with. Learning of her death in an airport restaurant via email, while we were en route for another travel weekend, left us undone. Unable to find the spirit of adventure abroad, we felt crumpled and worn. The airplane ride home for the memorial was long and tiring. At the beach house, the family connections ran deep as we shared stories and wine. We desperately missed our children, who were unable to be with us. We felt rushed, speeding through a time warp of memories, emotions, and new realities.

The five-year romp abroad gave us memories, friends, and experiences. Living and working internationally was one of the best decisions we've made as a couple. But while it was great in many ways, we had grown weary of the overseas lifestyle, realizing we were not career expats, but lucky travelers ready to go home. It was finally time to listen to the signals of being homesick, and then to act on them.

In our final month abroad, with bags already packed, a close friend called to share the devastating news of the unexpected death of her husband. When this strong woman tearfully asked in a broken voice, "Please, please, can you come home?," we knew we had made the right decision.

*Yvonne Ricketts, a native of Monterey, California is enjoying semi-retirement back in Monterey. She, along with her husband Randy, taught 7 years overseas in Jakarta, Indonesia, Vilnius, Lithuania, and Buenos Aires, Argentina. Yvonne spent 15 years in pre K-12 teaching and administration, 12 years in county government and consulting, and 10 years in local colleges as an adjunct faculty member.*

# ALL MY NEW FRIENDS ARE NAKED AND UNDERWATER

*Sterling Johnson*

"Heya, Pearl, you want to go to the jjimjilbang?" I looked up at the somewhat goofy-looking chubby-faced man in front of me and reluctantly said, "Whoa, okay, sure, let's give it a try...I guess."

What is a jjimjilbang, you might be wondering, and why was I so reluctant to go to one? Well, a jjimjilbang is one of these little neighbourhood saunas in Korea where people basically go get naked and hang around and soak with other naked people of the same gender. Being North American and a little prudish about public nudity, I was apprehensive. What the heck actually went on in these places? Are they like orgy rooms or something? But as I was new to the country, as was my newfound friend from Buffalo, I figured I should channel my spirit of adventure. "What the heck?," I thought. Let's go "hang out" and get to know each other...while totally naked. I guess you can only really make friends by exposing yourself and being vulnerable, and last time I checked, public nudity seemed not to hide too much. So off we went in search of the logo with the three puffs of steam coming out of it. It wasn't far away.

At the front desk we did our best to communicate that we wanted to go in. Funds were paid and the attendants gave us each a baby blue shirt-and-shorts set. Women were also entering and getting a pink shirt-and-shorts set. The attendants directed us to our left; however, my friend starting walking to the right, the women's side, which caused the attendants to panic, each yelling, "No, no, no!" We went over to the correct gender side and prepared to "immerse" ourselves in a uniquely Korean experience.

We stepped through the doorway, going past a magical curtain. What appeared before us was a welcoming communal room. Men were getting naked and putting stuff in lockers, which was our cue to do the same. "All right, I thought, let's do this!" My new friend and I started talking about life in Asia as we disrobed. He was coming from Thailand and I was coming from China. He loved hockey, as did I, and so began a friendship. We casually strolled back into the main foyer, fully exposed to all, and then proceeded into the pool room.

The first section we entered was the shower area. In most cases, the unfamiliar pubes on the bar of soap in front of me would cause me to pause, reconsider and exit the premises, but seeing as this was new to me and the potential norm, I rinsed off the hairy remnants. There were some pesky hangers-on, but I got that bar pretty clean before lathering up my own body. "Maybe we should bring our own soap next time!" I exclaimed.

Next we surveyed the surroundings. It looked to be a fairly pleasing spa with several pools, each with Korean men of various ages. We swallowed our pride, surveyed our own genitalia, and strode to the pool in front of us. It was steaming!

"Snikeys!" my friend exclaimed as he descended into the water. "Children be damned!" I yelped in reply as I plunged into the sperm-destroying heat. This was one hot pool. There were thermometer gauges on the side of the pool lighting up like an old arcade machine that seemed to indicate "Really F-in' Hot: Proceed with Caution."

An elderly Korean man raised his apparently-in-the-process-of-being-dyed eyebrows disapprovingly at us as he calmly entered the pool. We gathered this was a place for relaxation and that chatter should probably be kept to a minimum. I nodded and smiled at him, but quickly rethought my action as it might be yet another cultural faux pas. What exactly was the etiquette in this aquatic environment?

The next pool we encountered was really exotic looking, as the water was green. It was a green tea pool. "Very Asian!" I said. It was one of the nicer, aesthetically-speaking, pools in the jjimjilbang. It was wooden and had a spout that spewed hot tea water. My friend, who said he had been a bit of a carpenter in the past, admired the intricate woodwork that had been done on the roof and exterior. It was like a mini-temple. We hopped in and had a relaxing soak and sit, drifting away a bit and closing our eyes as we began to further settle in to our surroundings. Clouds, space, puffs of steam, and beautiful landscapes floated through my mind.

However, upon opening my eyes again and returning to the current environment, the landscape was decidedly testicular. There were several men lying exposed on a bunch of hot stones in front of us. Maybe it's time to move on, I started thinking to myself.

Immediately behind us we heard some vigorous splashing. A man was gyrating wildly in another pool, as though prepping for a bizarre synchronized swimming routine. I encouraged my friend to check it out with me and took the initiative by going in first, thinking it was just another warm pool. It was quite the shock to my system to discover the intense frigidity of the water. I splashed and flopped wildly, much to the joy of my yet-to-be-submerged companion. This was the cold pool—the coldest pool I'd ever experienced. And I'm from Canada! Despite many a dip in the lakes of my homeland, I had never quite experienced a polar dip to this extreme. "Wowza!" I exclaimed, recovering from my near-hypothermia-inducing ordeal.

After a quick trip to a fairly standard "dry" and "wet" sauna and some further conversation about hockey ("Go Jets!" "Go Sabres!"), we decided to go farther into the maze-like complex known as the jjimjilbang. We exited the pool area, toweled off, put on our baby blue pajamas and descended into the bowels of the building.

After going down a level, we wandered around, looking into the different rooms. We came upon what looked like a cross between a pizza oven and a teepee and decided to venture in for what we assumed would be one heck of a sweat. Inside, we were immediately struck by the almost ceremonial atmosphere suggested by the structure's exterior. It was quiet and of mixed gender. A man rocked and hummed silently in the corner in a primitive-sounding chant. All were sweating. I thought the pools before were hot, but this was a more deep, intense, desert-type heat. We followed the decorum of the place, closing our eyes while the heat took over our bodies. After several minutes of soaking through our baby blue PJs, by simply locking eyes and orienting them towards the exit, we took ourselves and our sweat back into the main common room. In this area, some would sleep through the night, families of three generations would catch up on the week's events, couples would snuggle without directly touching, and two hairy North Americans would learn more about each other while trying not to violate any other norms of jjimjilbang culture.

We were both feeling quite dehydrated and delirious, so thankfully there were little water dispensers scattered around the room. We greedily chugged from the tiny triangular paper cups provided, refilling a few times to replace a small fraction of the $H_2O$ that had just escaped our bodies. By the time we found those kind of airport lounge insert-a-dollar massage chairs, our PJs had almost fully dried. Our 1000 won bills bought ten minutes of back relaxation and staccato-filled conversation.

After the massage chairs, it was time to get on with our lives. As we re-robed, we agreed that despite the peculiarities, the jjimjilbang was actually a nice place to relax and have a good chat. We became regulars and grew to appreciate the quirky nature of the place. We got used to the intense heat of the pools and the teepee room. We accepted the soap situation. We appreciated the green tea and the blue pajamas. More importantly, in more ways than one, we learned to become comfortable in our own skin. Friendship truly is all about exposure, and when you can share what is light and what is dark about you (and what is big and not-so-big) with a non-judgmental human being, you can count yourself lucky.

*Sterling Johnson is originally from Winnipeg, Manitoba, Canada. He has taught internationally for 13 years in China, Korea and Malaysia. Sterling currently resides and teaches in Cairo, Egypt with his wife. They have two young children. Sterling is a middle school drama teacher.*

# SETTLING IN
*Allison Ritchie*

I'm in the back of a Landcruiser holding on to the handles so tightly that my knuckles are turning white. There are three other passengers, some doing the same as me, some cheering in delight. I see only sand and the back of the seat in front of me. A man in a kandura, the long white robe worn by Arab men, and a white headscarf is speeding up sand dunes, then slamming on the brakes to slide and skid until the vehicle feels like it will roll down the dune, end over end. Rihanna is blaring on the radio, not traditional Arabic music. My husband and I, along with the other new teachers, arrive safely but shakily at an oasis in the desert.

We are treated to a few activities, including sandboarding (like snowboarding but much slower), more dune bashing in the Landcruiser, and camel rides. The camels are surprisingly enormous. Climbing on one, I need to hold on tightly as it stands first on its hind legs, jerking me forward, then using its front legs to finally stand. Looking down, the ground is much further down than my comfort level. As the sun sets, the man leading my camel stops to break his fast with some dates. It is Ramadan, the month of fasting during daylight hours. Our arrival to our new home coincides with the end of this holy month. As a show of respect, we are told to refrain from eating or drinking in front of others during the day when we are out in public. After night falls, the copious amounts of lamb kofta, hummus, and arabic sweets consumed at dinner encourages our peaceful slumber under the desert stars.

How did we get here? I distinctly remember saying when recruiting, "anywhere but the Middle East." Yet here we were, dune bashing and camping in the Emirati desert.

Many things about the UAE initially shocked me, the immediate, intense heat and humidity being first and foremost. This was *not* going to be an easy place to settle in. Despite the heat and discomfort of being in an unfamiliar place, I was determined to follow the advice given during orientation: "make your home your own."

In Venezuela, I had not lived out those words. There, I adopted the "I'm not sure how long I will be here" attitude. My apartment walls in Maracaibo stayed mostly barren—not one picture was hung up until the middle of the school year. Instead of spending the extra dozen or so dollars on nicer things, I bought the cheapest products possible, including the toaster I replaced several times because it kept breaking.

This move to the UAE would not be like this. I would buy better quality items, decorating the way I wanted right away. Comfort items like cozy throws and pillows dotted the living room. Frames filled with pictures of "home" lined our apartment walls just days after moving in. A fancy toaster, one that would reliably pop up a minute after the lever was pressed down, perched comfortably on the kitchen counter alongside our new state-of-the-art blender and stainless steel knives.

"Make your home your own." I realized this advice was specifically referring to our apartment, but this new city was also my home.

I started exploring Abu Dhabi by car. Getting a license was relatively easy, aside from having to prove that my New Mexico driver's license was, in fact, from a part of the US, not a part of a neighboring country. Driving on the other hand, was full of unwanted thrills, my knuckles often white from the extra pressure of hands clutched to the steering wheel. However, the fright of navigating the roads was worth the freedom of seeing my new home city.

The Sheikh Zayed Mosque tour was one of those opportunities to explore. The mosque itself is one of the most beautiful pieces of architecture I have ever seen. The marble is blindingly white, especially with the intense sun and blue sky as a backdrop. Flowery vines made of abalone and mother of pearl inlay snake up the columns. Incredibly large chandeliers hang from the ceiling, shimmering with Swarovski crystals. A girl in her early twenties toured us around, telling us how 40,000 worshippers can be there at once, directing us to gaze at one of the largest carpets in the world, and informing us that the axis of the building is pointing toward Mecca. She encouraged us to ask questions, her answers teaching us not only information about the mosque, but also about life as an Emirati woman. We learned that wearing an *abaya* is frequently a woman's choice: some wear it, others do not. She stated with pride, "You can't tell how my body is under here, if I'm fat or thin, so it is left to the imagination." Our guide shared her experiences with things like marriage. Her parents had approved of many suitors, but she had not been fond enough of any of them to make the final decision. She talked about how the Sheik respected other religions and that there are multiple churches in the city.

Christmas was celebrated and trees were put up in malls and hotels. Our questions seem naive to me now, but I basically knew nothing about the culture at the time. In fact, I was the one who had to look up where the UAE is on a world map *after* we accepted our jobs.

In the weeks that followed, my eyes were opened to the amazingly diverse variety of food this new home had to offer. When I needed a tasty snack, there was a window where Afghan men stuck dough in a cylindrical hole, heating it up to the point where you had to wait a moment before eating, each precious second feeling the tension rise between risking a burnt inner mouth and delaying the gratification of the doughy goodness. When I needed comfort food, the train station-like building with cheeseburgers, fries, and shakes welcomed me with open arms. When I needed a change of pace, bubbly-fueled three-hour buffets at immaculate hotels did the trick. And I when I needed some crispy bread at home on a lazy Saturday morning, I had a fancy toaster that would brown each piece to perfection...every time.

In my first few months in Abu Dhabi, I learned that I need to feel comfortable in my own space. I also need to sometimes feel uncomfortable outside of it. I need family photos on the wall and throw pillows on the couch. I need to get lost and be unsure if what I just ate can technically be defined as "food." I need to ask locals questions. I need to hear their answers.

Am I settled? Maybe one day I fully will be, but then again maybe I won't. Regardless, the transition is always part of the adventure. And there are better ways to begin each one. The move to Abu Dhabi taught me how to "lean in" to the transition, to embrace it fully with arms open wide rather than extended straight ahead, keeping everything at arm's length.

*Allison Ritchie, a native of Farmington, New Mexico currently teaches in Doha, Qatar. She has taught middle school math for 17 years, 6 in the United States, and 11 in Venezuela, the United Arab Emirates, and Qatar.*

# THE TIME IS RIGHT FOR REVOLUTION
## *Andrew W. Jones*

When we first accepted international teaching jobs in Istanbul, I couldn't have been more excited. We were headed to one of the world's greatest cities to bop from one side of the famed Bosphorus to the other, hear the call to prayer boom into our stratosphere five times a day, and sip tea in tulip-shaped glasses—all part of opening our eyes to a new world. But it was my wife who pointed out the fine print in our contract—and indicated that my eyes would be seeing a most foreign sight in the mirror in Turkey: a clean-shaven face.

That's because Turkey, founded on secular principles by Mustafa Kemal Atatürk nearly a century earlier, had strict rules about beards in education. Beards, it was decreed, were Islamist. Beards meant *imams* preaching about the Koran. Beards represented the religious past of Turkey, and Atatürk was determined to move the country forward.

As such, facial hair was completely banned in our Turkish school for both teachers and students. And while a western reader might think, "Come on, this has to be the kind of rule that no one enforces," that would be wrong. It was enforced—diligently enforced—by the no-nonsense dean of students who roamed the halls, razor in hand, ready to send her next victim to the boys' bathroom to shave. As a result of her fervent desire to make Atatürk smile in his grave, it wasn't uncommon for me to walk into the bathroom and see teenage boys hacking away at their faces with cheap razors...and no shaving cream. Nicked and bleeding, they'd return to class humbled, with their heads down, several minutes later.

After one clean-shaven year of teaching under my belt, I'd escaped this bloody fate, but at the same time, I was sick of shaving—and ready to tempt fate. In a country that has essentially never had a revolution, I thought maybe, just maybe, the time was right. Because while I understood Atatürk's fears about the country slipping back into Islamist ways—this is, after all, where current president Recep Tayyip Erdoğan has been steering Turkey—I failed to see how a white dude from the Midwest with a ginger-y beard was really going to be a threat to anyone's republic. I showed up to the first day of teacher meetings in Year Two with the beard I'd been happily growing in America all summer. The facial hair rule, I knew, didn't go into effect until students actually showed up at school, so I didn't think my beard would make too many waves initially. But still, I was hoping to set an early tone: it was time to bring the beards back.

Little did I know that two other white dudes from the Midwest, as well as a New Yorker and a Canadian, felt the same way. So, on the first day of work, all thoughts of pedagogy were dumped into the Bosphorus. The five of us bearded fellows met and agreed the time had come: it was time for the beard revolution. As humorous as this sounds, when we met for the first time in an upstairs office with the door closed, there was no laughter coming from below our mustaches. The phrase "action plan" was used repeatedly. Mentions of "talking points" were sprinkled in, with a clear focus on "knowing the boundaries" and "taking control of the dialogue."

A strategy was hammered out: keep the beards trimmed nice and neat for teacher meetings, let our faces speak more than our words, don't level any ultimatums, encourage Turkish teachers to join us. Short of putting our hands together as one and belting out, "TEAM!" as a show of solidarity, we all strode out of that initial meeting feeling stronger. Our revolution was afoot—or, more fittingly, abeard. Gillette blades locked in our medicine cabinets, we were ready to fight this Turkish battle.

While the no-beard rule had originally stemmed from Atatürk's secular leanings, it became stringently enforced in the early 1980s during a time of great political strife in Turkey. Apparently, at that time, facial hair was used as a symbol of identity; people were being shot in the streets because of the styles of their beards or mustaches. Your facial hair indicated which political party and ethnicity you allied yourself with. Clearly, the symbolism behind this was serious.

On the flip side of this, the fact that I'd had a beard for the previous ten years had little to do with any larger statement...I just liked having a beard. This was, after all, my normal look.

But it wasn't my normal look in Turkey.

As I returned to school, I had expat male teachers sort-of-awkwardly talking to me about the handsomeness of my beard, male Turkish teachers wanting to chat grooming strategies, expat female teachers nodding to my wife with approval and saying, "Yes, he looks good," and Turkish female teachers telling me earnestly, "You should fight to keep this. Please, fight this fight."

The simple decision to challenge the rules brought comments from our Turkish colleagues that ran the gamut. One Turkish male sporting a summer-only beard told us in impassioned tones that he didn't feel like himself without his beard; his self-esteem plummets every time he has to shave. On the other end of the spectrum, another male proudly declared his allegiance to Atatürk and said he'd be damned if he let the country stray from its founding principles with our foolish designs on having beards.

But still, numerous Turks commented that while they liked what we were doing, we should probably prepare to shave it off soon. They'd seen this song-and-dance before. "It's nice you are trying this," a Turkish PE teacher said, "but you will shave it soon. You'll see how things work here."

All week rumors swirled around school about the fate of our beards. We Founding Five spoke in hushed tones in the hallways, whispered to each other during lunch, and stroked our beards while nodding to each other during staff meetings. It was as if we were a part of a secret club—except it was a pretty open secret. The furriness sprouting from our chin was not to be hidden. With each new day, we felt the momentum building but still, we knew this was Turkey. It's a country that has no problem bringing the hammer down on any momentum. Though Atatürk and Erdoğan had entirely opposite visions of what modern Turkey should be, they shared a similar fondness for strongman tactics in dealing with dissent. And we were well aware that we were working at a school that had no qualms about sending boys to the bathroom with a Bic and no shaving cream.

Amidst all this noise, our main talking point with the school's administration was simple: our beards aren't statements; they're just who we are. This is the same argument that polarizes Turkey over women wearing the headscarf. Those in favor say the exact same thing: the headscarf isn't a statement; it's just who we are. On the other hand, liberals say that women not wearing headscarves aren't making statements either; they're just being who they are. This debate started with Atatürk 100 years ago, continues with Erdoğan today, and shows no signs of abating.

As a realist, I figured our beard revolution might have us digging into the trenches and battling this out for quite a while. But then, eight days into our revolution, with five days remaining before the first day of school, one of the Founding Five, a Wisconsinite with a somewhat disheveled gray goatee, came up to me and patted me on the back just before the day's first meeting.

"We won," he beamed. "Beards are in."

"What? You're kidding."

"Nope," he kept smiling. "Put away your razors. Go buy that beard trimmer. We're wearing our beards this year."

"Just like that? I mean, I can't believe it happened without a bigger fight."

"It was time," he said, pausing for dramatic effect. "It was time for our voices to be heard."

He might've been joking. But looking at the pride emanating from his face (not just his beard), I couldn't see any levity. After all, this was our revolution.

Maybe it was a revolution that was a long time coming. Both our school and the country were ready to move into the 21st century. Or maybe it was the exact opposite: the school knew that the Islamist Erdoğan would approve of a relic from the past: bearded teachers. Or maybe the administration caved to the power of a revolution, a finely trimmed and neatly coiffed revolution whose action plan and talking points were just too powerful to rebut.

For whatever reason, the decision had been made: beards were back. Next, in true Turkish revolutionary spirit, it was clear what would follow. "So what do you think about this earring?" the Wisconsinite offered, turning his ear my way. "I think this should be our next battle. Do you think they'll let me wear it?"

*Andrew W. Jones, a native of Downers Grove, Illinois, teaches in Brasilia, Brazil. He has taught high school English for 17 years—8 in the US and 9 in Bulgaria, Ecuador, Turkey, and Brazil.*

# ALL THE TIME IN THE WORLD
*Alicia Ritter*

On a pollution-free Sunday in Shanghai, my eight-year-old daughter and I were headed to Shanghai Disney. That particular morning we grabbed a blueberry smoothie as we passed our favorite little Australian coffee joint, then headed toward the great day ahead. I told my daughter to wait on the sidewalk while I walked across the bike lane in order to hail a cab from the street. Sometimes these bike lanes double as a sidewalk or scooter lane, the rules often blurred so much there are basically no rules—just walk, ride, and drive wherever you want. As I saw a cab slowing down, there were no scooters or bikes in sight, so I motioned for my daughter to come join me at the cab. Suddenly I noticed something quick and black in my peripheral vision. Out of nowhere, a scooter was flying towards us in the middle lane. I looked at my daughter and saw it all happening in slow motion. If she took just one more step, at the rate the scooter was going, it was evident they would collide. I screamed from a few feet away, watching helplessly as she stepped out and was hit.

In an instant the scooter turned sideways, remnants of a smoothie splattered across twenty feet of pavement, and a motionless child was lying on the ground. There was no one to help, except for the security guard standing outside a furniture store who witnessed the accident. His duty, however, was to guard the furniture store. Never mind that that shop was closed and wouldn't open for another three hours, he was to stand guard outside the shop unless someone higher up told him differently. Screaming mothers, fallen scooters, and unconscious children didn't fall into that category.

For seconds I heard a ringing in my ears—then everything fell silent in my world, including my child. I began screaming hysterically, running in slow motion toward where, just one second earlier, my eight-year-old girl had been simply walking along the sidewalk, singing and wearing her white dress printed with soft blue and pink flowers. Now, here she was, tossed several feet from the impact of the blow, lying motionless on the pavement.

Miraculously, she began moving on her own. Covered in blood, she started crawling out of the way of the bikes and scooters that were now beginning to pass. Though there was a look of sheer terror in her eyes and tears streaming down her face, she immediately scolded me, telling me to stop screaming. With the taxi door still open, the driver didn't know what to do. About this time, an American girl casually strolled by to get in the taxi.

I was in utter shock, stunned that she would even dare to walk past this incident and grab our cab. "Excuse me," I said catching up to her. "Excuse me!"
"What?"
"I was about to use this taxi—we need it to go to the hospital," I said, pointing to my child on the sidewalk.

"Um...I actually called this taxi. This is my taxi," she said in a tone I will never forget. "There will be another one that comes along soon. Chill out."

Here in my head I had been criticizing the Chinese guard and taxi driver, but the arrogance and indifference of the American woman showed me that common sense and empathy were lacking in both cultures at this moment.

The lady who had been driving the scooter, however, immediately came to my daughter's aid. She was sitting with her the moment I stepped away to confront the taxi thief, and I could tell she was genuinely apologetic. The rule in China is that if you accidentally hit someone, you have to pay for their medical expenses. This woman spoke no English but took responsibility. She offered to drive us on her scooter to our hospital of choice. The foreign medical clinic we used would have likely been too expensive to treat this on a cash basis. I told her in Chinese to take us to whichever hospital she felt comfortable with. To get to the hospital, my daughter and I had to ride on the same bike that caused the tragedy moments earlier.

She first drove us to her house. Though it wasn't far away, it seemed as if we were the first foreigners the neighborhood had seen in a while—or ever—by the way people looked at us as they came in and out of the front gate. She told us to wait next to a taxi while she went upstairs. I began to wonder if she was coming back down, or if this was her way of escaping, but she returned with a wad of pink Renminbi in hand. "Zou ba." She said to the driver. "Let's go."

At the hospital there were lines upon lines of people. You took a number, though probably due to the appearance of a girl in a blood-stained dress we were moved through the line a bit faster. There are procedures, though, at Chinese hospitals. Before you get treated, you go through several rooms and steps, including payment first, before they check for weight, height, and temperature. These might be the equivalent of checking vitals in the United States, but in the ER I expected they might skip measuring the height of an injured child. After the initial screenings, patients seemed to be treated in five minutes or less.

I could see why the procedures were happening so quickly. There was no change of the sheets nor the white paper on the table from the person before. My daughter was plopped on the table, laid down, and then a nurse held her while a doctor started pouring peroxide over the wounds. My daughter immediately began to cry as they quickly grabbed swabs of cotton and gauze to clean out the wounds as rapidly as possible. I couldn't watch. I held her hand and told her to be still.

No stitches were needed, as luckily everything appeared to be on the surface. They closed and protected the wounds with amazing speed, working as efficiently as a NASCAR pit crew. Within minutes we were done. Next! The succeeding patient was escorted in as the bloody paper stayed on the treatment room table.

The woman got a taxi for us and took us back home. She offered to give me the rest of her wad of cash, but I said no. She still seemed nervous, almost as if she would have felt better if we had taken the money, but money was not what I cared about: I was relieved that we were back home and everyone was alive. I thanked her and we parted ways. My daughter couldn't have gotten hit by a nicer person. On our way home we stopped by the Australian coffee shop and got a fresh blueberry smoothie.

The next day I stayed at home with my daughter just to make sure there were no internal injuries. Everything seemed fine, and she even had a piano recital that night. On a typical day, as a busy working mom, I might have gotten her changed for the recital in a bathroom stall moments before performance time, brushing her hair in a hurry, bobby pins clenched between my teeth. But on that day, I had all the time in the world to curl her hair, put a little makeup on her, and look at my beautiful girl. She wore a different white dress that night, covering the wounds beneath, and she played flawlessly.


*Alicia Ritter, a native of Dallas, Texas, currently teaches in Shanghai, China. She has taught for fifteen years, 5 in the US, and 10 abroad in Beijing, Abu Dhabi, and Shanghai. Her daughter will be receiving her 50th stamp in her passport this year and now looks both ways before crossing the street.*

# CHAIN MIGRATION
*Kevin A. Duncan*

"Picante." "Pi-can-te!" Three-year-old Lia Trotter knows a little Spanish and a little English…but I'm pretty sure she doesn't know which is which when she utters these words. It is 2009 and we are in my favorite Indian restaurant in suburban Seoul, complete with air conditioning strong enough to fight the intense heat and humidity of a Korean August. I've known Lia since she was just a couple of months old. Her father Tim and I were new teachers at the Country Day School in suburban San Jose, Costa Rica, while her mother Jen was getting her master's degree at the University for Peace a few miles down the road. Sitting across from me is Gabriel, Lia's younger brother. Born half a year ago, with locks of hair desperately trying to escape his head, Gabriel is too young to say any Spanish words from his birthplace.

Next to them, eating the same samosas and curries but not finding them nearly as spicy as Lia, are newlyweds Michael and

Marisol, now sharing a last name. Ten days prior, the Jobes tied the knot on a beautiful Costa Rican beach. Their "honeymoon" began less than 36 hours later, flying from Costa Rica to Korea just in time to join Lia's parents in starting new teacher orientation at the school where I have been working for a year. To throw down the "Welcome to Korea" mat and catch up on my former school and trips to the volcanoes and beaches I left behind, I welcome them in an unusual manner: by eating Indian food at my favorite restaurant. This christening of former Costa Rica teachers into their new lives by tasting the best garlic naan in Korea is supposed to be a one-time event. Much to my surprise, it ends up becoming a multi-year tradition.

A few weeks earlier at Michael and Marisol's July wedding on a picturesque tropical beach, the bride's hair stylist did wonderful work but was the opposite of efficient. The extra coiffure time allowed for a long conversation between yours truly and another couple—Steve and Miriam Katz—still living in Costa Rica. He, a tech integration teacher from California with an iconic beard who had been podcasting long before it was "cool," and his beautiful wife, a Costa Rican who taught Spanish to US university students studying abroad, were thinking of moving their family abroad if the right opportunity presented itself. As the wedding crowd patiently waited for Marisol to appear, and as the Pacific Ocean breeze made the sun's rays feel more innocuous than my pale skin would later demonstrate them to be, the Katzes grilled me on the pros and cons of living and working in an Asian city with a population four times that of Costa Rica.

"What's it like living in Seoul?"

"Well, to be honest, I had culture shock coming back to Costa Rica. There's so much space here...there are buildings that aren't even high-rises. But every teacher in Seoul does get a MacBook."

"Every teacher? A MacBook?"

"Yes, of course."

"Sold!"

Twelve months later, Steve and Miriam and their two children are half a world away from Costa Rica, eating tasty veggie curries in the same wonderfully air-conditioned Indian restaurant with all the other Costa-Rica-to-Korea veterans: the Trotters, the Jobes, and myself. Lia is there again, having forgotten how to say "picante" and most of her other Spanish words, but at least knowing which foods to avoid this time. Her baby brother Gabriel now has a full head of hair and, despite not yet knowing how to express himself in Korean, is already developing a tolerance for the distinct spiciness of Korean food. As the palak paneer is passed around the table, the Katzes, the new family, learn from us how to hike to school from their apartment and the importance of importing ingredients from abroad. They return the favor by sharing news of former students and colleagues, update us on the locals' thoughts on the new Costa Rican president, and give us the latest gossip on our friend Jason who decided to take a sabbatical year.

"Jason's going to spend a month hiking the Camino de Santiago in Spain."

"When?"

"About the time we'll be doing progress reports and holding parent/teacher conferences."

"Oof. Well, good for him...Does he have other big plans throughout the year?"

"He'll either be in the caves of Turkey, the hills of Austria, or the mountains of Morocco while we're finishing our end of semester report cards...he's going to play it by ear."

"Well at least we get a few days off for Christmas."

With stomachs slightly distended from over-ordering and with garlic seeping through our pores, we step back into the Korean heat, thankful that we can fondly connect to our old lives and share stories and advice from our new ones.

Months pass; it's my third year in Korea, the Trotters and Jobes' second, and the Katzes' first. We manage to feel the intense summer heat turn into a far too long winter, the prospect of spring teasing us for what feels like a whole year. Finally, in May, spring emerges. After spending his sabbatical traveling in Spain, Morocco, Hungary, Croatia, Thailand, and beyond, Jason ends his year away from teaching by visiting us in Korea. When he arrives, we're only slightly jealous of him for traveling the world while we were stuck with alarm clocks, weekend grading, and snowy sidewalks. He experienced so much in his year abroad, but we've also changed quite a bit since we were all last together two years prior at Michael and Marisol's wedding. Jason can't believe how much Lia and Gabriel have grown. He can't believe how much weight I've gained by eating McDonald's double bulgogi burgers, how well the Katzes have adapted to their new country, and that Michael and Marisol are expecting twins in a few months. He also can't believe how much he enjoys the Korean spring, Korean baseball games, and the new people he has met. So when an unexpected opportunity arises at the last minute to teach grade five at our school starting in August, he jumps at the chance.

Three months later, we're all eating papadum and cooling our mouths with yogurt desserts at the same delightfully chilled restaurant. Four years in a row of Costa Rica transplants, and three years in a row of the "Welcome to Korea" Indian meal tradition. This time we don't have to teach the new person—Jason—about day-to-day living in Seoul, but we do still talk about all the times that baby Lia made the trip with us to the Poas Volcano Lodge in Costa Rica, how much I sweated while dancing at Michael and Marisol's wedding, and how crazy it is that we all ended up in Korea.

In some ways, I completely understand why we all ended up here. In my opinion, all of the Costa-Rica-to-Korea crew are not only great people, but also excellent colleagues. The principals and school directors in Korea appreciated hearing a positive "inside scoop" before offering these strangers a two-year teaching contract. As one administrator said, "Hiring is challenging, you never really know what you're going to get." Getting inside information from people like me helped school leaders feel confident that Lia's parents and the others around that table were far more likely to be Godiva- and Ferrero Rocher-quality instead of turning out to be Milk Duds.

"This Tim Trotter guy was a Navy pilot AND was a nationally ranked judo competitor?"

"Yes. I don't think you'll have discipline issues in his class."

Although I had put in a good word for the others who sat under the intricate tapestries of elephants and Ganesh every August, many other things had to fall into place besides positive recommendations and quality candidates applying. The positions had to be available in the right year, at the right time in the hiring season, and at the right school. Connections alone are certainly not a guarantee of anyone getting a job. As much as I might try to work with some people again, it's often not meant to be. However, sometimes the chain migration from point A to point B continues even without effort.

"Hello Jim, I'm Kevin." "Hi, I'm Marisol." "I'm Michael." "I'm Jason." And so on, as we go around the table, mango lassis in hand, waiting for the tandoori chicken to arrive. Now for five years in a row, teachers from Costa Rica have come to Korea, and for the last four, their first stop has been to eat at Thali with veterans of that move. Our newest member is Jim, an incoming high school English teacher, someone none of us know. He taught at our previous school for just two years, starting after the rest of us had moved on. Jim is a stranger to us, but the move from Central America to East Asia is not.

We've all changed since our time in Costa Rica, partly due to the natural process of growing older and also due to the fact that we're living in Korea. Lia has started school, and Gabriel can now run, his flowing locks trailing behind as evidence of this newfound skill. Their father Tim, who is half-Korean, now knows his long lost relatives and their mother Jen has settled in to her new role teaching in the learning support center. Steve Katz is now an Apple Distinguished Educator, his wife Miriam has adjusted from teaching university students to teaching at the primary and secondary levels, and their Costa-Rican born kids are now in middle school. Michael and Marisol's ten-month-old twins are finally on the same sleep schedule, and Jason has become skilled at all types of golf in Korea (screen golf, "park golf," par-three pitch and putt, frisbee) though he still dreams of life without alarms. As for me, I have dropped ten kilos, thanks in part by cutting my Double Bulgogi Burger consumption by approximately 97%.

But alas, traditions overseas can vanish almost as quickly as they begin. At the end of Jim's first year, our large Costa-Rica-to-Korea crew is once again gathered around the same table at Thali, but instead of saying "welcome," we are saying "farewell." I am heading to China to dip my toes into the IB teaching world. Michael, Marisol, and their twins are heading to Singapore to begin a new adventure as a young family. For the first time, our group is getting smaller. Over the next few years, Lia and Gabriel's family will move to Turkey, the inquisitive Katzes and their kids will move to Malaysia, Jason will take another gap year before moving to Singapore, and Jim will return to the US.

In less than ten years, the Costa-Rica-to-Korea chain migration will begin, expand, contract, and end. At the Korea International School, other pipelines of teachers from schools in Kuwait and Jordan will form, while the Costa-Rica-to-Korea one will be largely forgotten, much like Lia's Spanish. But neither of these new chains will greet newcomers by gathering around a table in that highly air-conditioned Indian restaurant in suburban Seoul, sharing memories of life near volcanoes and beaches while eating South Asian food, both mild and picante.

*Kevin A. Duncan, a native of Columbia, Tennessee, teaches in Buenos Aires, Argentina. He has taught high school social studies for 17 years, 4 in the US and 13 in Costa Rica, South Korea, China, and Argentina.*

# THE YARD
*Jesse Howe*

The blazing mid-August sun is already high overhead at 10:00 a.m. as I drive into the *fútbol* complex through rusted metal gates. The cinder-block walls stand five meters high and are topped with broken bottles, an infallible security system common throughout the developing world. I spot my contact Luis, a greying custodian from our school, as he collects pesos at the entrance. He acknowledges my arrival with a toothy grin and a fist bump, then admits he didn't think I would show. *"Por qué?"* I ask. His gaze slowly disengages from mine as his dark brown eyes wander toward the scene that unfolds before us. There are three pitches, none of which has more than a few blades of grass sprouting from the dust and dirt, accompanied by various divots that affect the movement of tattered soccer balls. Anything light enough to be picked up and carried away by the hot desert air swirls into mini-tornadoes. I survey my surroundings and imagine watch towers on the four corners with shotgun-toting prison guards securing 'the yard' at a penitentiary. Mexican *banda* music with its staccato style of percussion and horns, popular with the local *norteños*, blares from makeshift grill stations. I spot *carne asada* (grilled beef), but in a hat tip to the blue-collar nature of the players and fans, the aroma that wafts past our nostrils is the cheaper, more pungent *higado* (liver). Revelry always permeates the air of these fields, accompanied by the rattle and clink of beer bottles, shouts of *"GOL!,"* and the occasional fist fight. The yard is a total assault on the senses, a completely different world from the quiet green playing fields and manicured lawns at the elite private school where I teach.

At the onset of my second year at Colegio Americano de Torreón, I began to tire of surface-level interactions with locals. Those interactions had always left me wanting more: community involvement, a local pub, pro team season tickets. This desire for more prompted my search for a local soccer team. I began to spread the word among local school staff. It's not that it took me a full year to find a team; I already had one full season under my belt with *"Los Diplomaticos,"* a team of fellow expat teachers. It's that I yearned to play with a team of locals, a team of Mexicans. Fortuitously a member of the school's maintenance staff answered my query.

This particular league is for those aged 35 and over, and I barely qualify. The age bracket explains the absurd prevalence of beer bellies and grey hair. Luis quickly introduces me to members of my team and hustles back to his perch. As I sit down to lace up my cleats, my teammates look at me with a certain amount of skepticism: after all, *gringos* aren't exactly known for their skill at playing sports with their feet. I am certain I am the first and only foreigner to receive an invite to play at the yard. *"Gringo, donde juegas?"* The team captain barks in my direction, asking my position. *"Yo juego en la defensa, de central,"* I reply with conviction. As a central defender in a 4-4-2 formation, I pair with the darkest member of our team, *el negro* they call him. Among the things held in high regard by Mexicans are the well-known trio of family, football, and beer. Lesser known is their affinity for nicknames. Among my teammates there are also *Zurdo* (Lefty), *Payaso* (Clown), and *Chino* (Curly). My teammates christen our partnership '*sal y pimienta*' (salt and pepper) due to our contrasting complexions, and we form a fast friendship on and off the field.

The referee's whistle blows to signify the start of my first game, and with it comes a blitz of attacking football from our opposition. The out-of-shape body movements on the pitch are incongruent with their grace and skill on the ball; I am reminded that they had all grown up with balls at their feet and I had not. Nevertheless, I hold my own on the back line with several blocked shots, clearances, and a well-placed elbow or two. *Negro* and I anchor the defense and do our best to hold off the onslaught, but eventually we concede a goal. It is the only goal scored during the game, and with it begins our streak of winless football.

Our team was unique in that we were sponsored by the proprietor of the grounds, an older bespectacled fellow who occasionally joined us on the field but never once covered himself in glory. Later in the season there was a heated post-game conversation between the two of us in which I informed him that the reason we had played well and won the game was because he had remained on the bench. The snickers of my disbelieving teammates spoke volumes. Despite our sponsor's shortcomings as a soccer player, other benefits existed: not only did he cover our inscription fees, but he also paid for the first case of post-game beers. Only later in the season, when our losing streak reached unprecedented levels, did he threaten to cut off our post-match beer supply. Never did I see a team in such low spirits after he actually followed through. No matter who paid, these men held true to the time-honored mantra, "Win or lose, we still booze."

Sundays are sacred in Torreón, not only for the sacrament but also for the blood, sweat, and tears spilled on the pitch. Sundays in the yard represented a release from the pressures and hardships faced by the working-class Mexicans who were my teammates, every one of whom I am honored to call *mi amigo*. My style of physical play, which earned a fair share of yellow and red cards that season, was well received, and I was always met with a friendly greeting of *"Gringo!"* upon arrival.

Five years have passed since that first game at the yard. My desire for a more authentic Mexican experience has been more than fulfilled.

*Jesse Howe, a native of the Washington DC area, has taught in elementary schools for 8 years; 2 in the US and 6 in Mexico and Colombia. In 2019, he will continue to Chile. Jesse has fully embraced Latin American culture and continues to play soccer recreationally, savoring the rare goal he scores. He looks forward to introducing his young son Julian to the beautiful game.*

# TWO WORLDS: A POEM AND SOME MUSINGS
## *Tara Waudby*

Part I: A Poem

I am born under the willowy birch trees
of *Kungliga Skogen*; grow up on the mossy rocks
of this forest, running across meadows of sunny buttercups
waving at sailboats in the archipelago.

I am from *amerika*, with its gigantic supermarkets,
proud of my California Beach Bum t-shirt.
I brag about all the swag I see and know; they don't know
I have none of it. Too poor even for a hotel

on the way *home*. The time we slept at Victoria Station,
London, no food, until a nice gentleman bought us
one ham sandwich to quell my tears and my sister's.
The terror when the man reeking of drink

wedged between my mother and me, stroking her blond hair,
ignoring the two small brown girls beside crying,
*mamma, mamma.* Twenty years later,
I am from America! As Taiwanese grandmothers

stroke my arm in disbelief. Brazil! Argentina?
America! *amerika.* I am not from
where I'm from. I am born under a midnight sun,
raised under saguaro arms, aged across time zones.

I am from Everywhere. Nowhere.
I am not from where I'm from.

Part II: Some Musings

For years, I have envied the expats who come overseas with a
strong sense of place. They travel the world but still have a
hometown, a home culture. They build strong relationships and
stay connected with one another even when moving from
country to country.

In contrast, I feel I am from everywhere...and nowhere. My
parents are from two different countries, and I spent the first
ten years of my life in Sweden, a country that was neither of
their native homes, before moving to Phoenix, Arizona. And
while we were back in my mother's home country, Arizona was
not her home state; her family had relocated from South Dakota
in the years she had spent overseas. Once again we were
transplants in a foreign land, even if it partly was our own.

To my English husband, I am very American. But in America, I
have never felt American enough. Set aside the ever-constant
question, *Where are you from?,* which Americans love to ask to see
where one fits into the five standard boxes: Caucasian, Hispanic,
Native American, African-American, Asian or Pacific Islander. I

am also different because of things like my my word choice. As a mom of multicultural children, I find it easier to use a similar vocabulary in our household. Thus, trash has become rubbish. Elevator is lift. Pants are trousers. Dinner is tea. Well, I still can't call dinner tea, but I do use a more British vocabulary, one that sounds foreign in Arizona.

My envy of my expat colleagues, though, does not stem from vocabulary. It arises when I see how connected they remain, even as they shift across continents and time. Like many of my students, I am a TCK (Third Culture Kid). Recently, during a presentation about TCK students, I learned that TCKs disconnect easily and move around fluidly. It's not that I don't equally love or value my friendships, but it's just that this is how it has always been for me. You move. You move on. You cherish memories. You create new ones.

Perhaps though, what we TCKs seek is not to have one home, but an understanding of our many homes. *I am from everywhere. Nowhere.* The bluish midnight sky of Stockholm summers…the vibrant pinkish, reddish hues of Arizona sunsets…the flashing neon lights of Taichung night markets…the crescent moon that begins each new lunar cycle in the Arabian Gulf. These beautiful sights are all a part of me, but they are not all of who I am.

As TCKs like me produce our own TCKs, I hope the question begins to shift from *Where are you from?* to *Where have you been?* or *What makes you You?* I hope my daughters will be accepted not because they belong to one particular place, but because they are a part of so many. I hope that people will appreciate as much as I do that my daughters believe the best egg fried rice can be found at a small restaurant on Railay Beach in Krabi, Thailand…and that the second best, a close rival to Thailand's, is at a streetside restaurant in New York City's Chinatown…and that this is a conversation we revisit regularly as each daughter mourns the fried rice she may never eat again.

Whether we miss the fried rice or the people we leave as we travel from place to place, we honor the memories of where we've been. We TCKs may struggle with connection, but at the same time our connections to this world are abundant.

*We are from Everywhere. Nowhere.*
*We are not from where we're from.*

*Tara Waudby, a TCK born in Stockholm, Sweden, teaches in Bahrain. She has taught English, EAL, special education, and served as an administrator for 20+ years, 3 in the U.S. and the remainder overseas in Taiwan, Kuwait, Saudi Arabia and Bahrain.*

# ROSA OQUENDO SAYS HELLO
## *Brad Evans*

Much of what is significant in my life has largely been defined by the actions of a complete stranger nearly two decades ago. In the great chain of events that make up our lives, I can retrace some significant moments in my own chain to a single person. I've never met her nor has she met me. I have no idea where she is nor (mostly) where she has been, yet there is a great deal I owe her. And you owe her as well.

Without Rosa Oquendo, you would not be reading this book.

In the Spring of 2001, Matt Minor (yes, that one, from the book cover), the recent owner of a two-bedroom condo, was in his first year of teaching at a school in Deerfield, a suburb just north of Chicago. Thanks to the magic of a Craigslist classified ad, Rosa Oquendo and Matt had been roommates for several months. After meeting a wealthy financial trader in the city, she simply took off one day, never to return. She left a family photo album on the desk, heaps of clothes in the closet, and leopard-print sheets on the bed. Despite repeated attempts from Matt to have her pick up her stuff and pay the owed rent, Oquendo went radio silent for several years, leaving Matt with a spare room and an urgent need for a new tenant. On the school district's e-mail message board, he let the teachers know he had a room for rent. This led to an email conversation with Taf, perhaps the only other teacher in Deerfield who had even read the message. Matt was looking for a tenant for an entire year. Taf only needed a place for a couple of months.

Taf had just sold his townhome much earlier than anticipated. He was getting ready to leave the 'burbs of Chicago to start teaching in China. For the life of him, Matt couldn't figure out why anyone would leave the Cubs, deep dish pizza, or the stability of a top notch school district, but seeing as no one else was responding, he was glad to have *somebody* pay the rent, especially one who didn't mind the pepto bismol-pink spare bedroom neatly painted by his absent roommate. In their short time together, Matt and Taf developed a friendship that continued far beyond Taf's final months living in Chicago. For the next seven summers, Taf would come back to visit while also attempting to convince Matt, his friend and former landlord, to move abroad himself.

In 2008, Taf's persistence and encouragement finally paid off as Matt landed a job in Seoul, where in his first year he met his wife Cailin and made a new friend named Kevin Duncan, co-curator of this book. During this time I, also a Chicago native but with no idea who Matt or Taf were, graduated from college and got frustrated trying to find a teaching job during the Great Recession. Through friends I learned there were opportunities teaching English at tutoring academies or local schools in South Korea, so I started to plot my own move abroad for adventure and employment.

In 2010, one month after leaving the Chicagoland area, my mouth was getting used to the Korean gochujang spice and the ubiquitous kimchi, but I had yet to meet anyone I really connected with. My local school was tiny, and only a handful of people in the whole building could muster more than a "hello," "thank you," or "nice to meet you" in English.

Alone in Korea, I decided to sign up for a touristy weekend trip to an ice festival a few hours outside Seoul. If you've travelled even a little, you are aware of tour buses. They are often impersonal, unloading their cargo at each popular attraction like troops storming the beaches, fighting for the very best photo-op. I usually like to avoid them, having a bit of humanity-induced claustrophobia in such settings. But in this Korean January, there was no better way to see humongous ice sculptures and do a little ice fishing than by taking a group tour with 39 other strangers.

Not long before arriving the tour leader had all the passengers introduce ourselves. "Say your name and where you're from." We passed the microphone around: "I'm Brad from Chicago." "I'm Wu from Beijing." "I'm Stacy from London." "I'm Kevin from Tennessee." "I'm Matt from Chicago." My eyes darted to the front of the bus, but all I could see was the back of the Chicago guy's navy blue stocking cap.

The bus pulled into the well-salted parking lot. The door opened and the crew began unloading, pairs and large groups dressed in layers streaming out, ready to enjoy the icy attractions and each other's company. As for me, I was ready to take on the day by myself.

Taking the stairs off the bus into the cool Hwacheon air, I found Matt waiting outside for "the other guy from Chicago." I was wearing my blue Chicago Cubs stocking cap; he was wearing his navy Chicago Bears one. I didn't know how this weekend would go, but at least there was someone with a great taste in pro sports teams.

With strangers, conversations usually have a natural course: they begin broadly and eventually narrow to their smallest possible points. Some, if there's not much of a connection, end abruptly at "Oh, I've been to Chicago once," while others, as in this case, get narrower and narrower, even astonishingly so. It turned out that Matt had grown up in the suburb next to mine, had attended my rival school, and had coached baseball at my high school...while I was there! He knew many of the same people I had just seen a few weeks prior. It was like we were meeting each other at Booker's Bar & Grill in Elgin, Illinois instead of in a remote mountain village a few miles from the North Korean border.

Matt, being the thoughtful person he is, quickly invited me to join his friends and coworkers. Within minutes I had met the group from his school, riding ATVs on the ice with them and trying our (frostbitten) hand at barehanded ice fishing. That night the tour bus riders had to sleep in large rooms of nine people. Matt, Kevin, and his fellow teachers had space for one more. I ended up being the "9th wheel" as I didn't know anyone prior, but they made me feel like an equal part of the group.

Conversations over that weekend informed me about the greatest secret in education: international schools. International teaching sounded like the perfect blend of work and play, yet I did not know it existed until that weekend. There is no "International Schools and Teaching 101" I am aware of at any College of Education. No international teaching career counselors. It almost felt like it was being hidden from people like me. As a recently certified social studies teacher, I moved to Korea teaching English, a job that didn't require courses on pedagogy, assessment, and classroom management. It only required a college degree from an English-speaking university, a clean background check, and a pulse.

Returning from the ice festival, I continued to hang out with Matt, Kevin, and the others back in Seoul. I became friends with more people from their school who didn't go to the festival. Over the next few months, my friendship with this group developed as we played frisbee golf on homemade courses, bluffed our way through late night Texas Hold 'em games, and watched South Korea notch a World Cup victory against Greece.

When a maternity leave position to teach high school literature came open at the international school, the administration was happy to have a certified teacher already living in the country who was willing and able to take the job, even if my expertise was more Churchill and Stalin than MacBeth and Dostoyevsky. That temporary position turned into a permanent one as the school then hired me to teach middle school social studies beginning the next year. I would go on to work at that school in Seoul for the next five years.

In 2013, during my fourth year overseas, I met and started dating a cute, goofy new hire from Kansas City with her own causal chain leading her to work at the same school in Seoul. Flirtations led to dating and dating led to marriage. Not long after, Jen and I "put a ring on it," changed jobs, and moved to Shanghai. Taf, Matt's friend and former roommate from Chicago, was still there, sixteen years later. On day one of orientation with the returning teachers, I asked around and found Taf. I walked up to him without introducing myself and said: "Rosa Oquendo says hello."

Laughter erupted. Taf hadn't heard that name in years.

Taf and I weren't just connected because of Matt, our Chicago heritage, the fact that we were teaching at the same school, or our lack of hair; we and many others were connected because of one woman: Rosa Oquendo.

If Rosa Oquendo hadn't abruptly left that Pepto-pink bedroom sixteen years prior, then:

- Matt and Taf wouldn't have met and become close friends;
- Taf wouldn't have convinced Matt to move abroad;
- Matt wouldn't have met his wife in Korea, and they wouldn't have moved together to Thailand, Colombia, and China;
- Matt wouldn't have met Kevin in Korea (meaning this book wouldn't exist);
- I wouldn't have bumped into Matt, Kevin, and everyone else at the ice festival;
- I wouldn't have been introduced to the international school system;
- I wouldn't have gotten a job at their school in Seoul, or later in Shanghai at Taf's school, where Matt and his wife would join us the following year;
- and, most importantly for me, I wouldn't have met my wife.

Obviously, there are other variables that contributed to this chain of events, other things that impacted my decision-making and my journeys, whether it was something as large as a global recession or as small as wearing a Cubs hat instead of the other one in my closet.

We all have a version of Rosa Oquendo in our lives, perhaps even more than one, someone we may never know who has been immensely, perhaps inexorably, instrumental in our development, in who we have become. It's funny that my life in Shanghai—my job, my wife, my friends—can be traced back, link by link, to a seemingly rash decision by a stranger in Chicago nearly twenty years ago. And for that, in the off-chance she's reading this, I'd like to say, "Thank you, Rosa Oquendo, and hello."

*Brad Evans, originally from Chicago, Illinois, teaches in Shanghai, China. He has taught middle school social studies for 9 years in South Korea and China.*

# FINAL THOUGHTS

## ANOTHER ONE IN THE BOOKS
*Matt Minor*

When Dunc and I decided to curate our first book together two years ago, we knew it would be an adventure unlike any experienced in 64 combined countries of travel. We were energetic and naive. We had ideas and visions. We had no template and built the plane as we flew it. There were sleepless nights, frustrating setbacks, and doubts about whether we could really pull it off. However, we persevered and even managed to keep to Dunc's unwavering timeline. Though the process was more exhausting than anticipated, we called it a victory. Our friendship was still intact and the goal of publishing a book for charity had been achieved.

There's a term sometimes associated with childbirth called the "Halo Effect," where new mothers in the moment of holding their child for the first time often report that the pain experienced in labor just a few minutes earlier has all but been forgotten. The pride and joy of having a newborn help alleviate any memory of the preceding pain. As Dunc and I held our yellow, matte-finished softcover baby in our hands, we seemed to completely forget the struggles, frustrations, and hard work that it took to get there. Time passed, word spread, and a surprising number of books were sold. Like many proud parents, we started to consider another "edition" to the family.

Almost one year after the date of the book launch, Dunc and I were crafting another email to prospective authors looking for stories to fill a second volume. This time around, we knew the long road ahead, yet still proceeded. We were gluttons for punishment.

To be fair, there were a lot of great reasons to curate a second volume. First off, through sales and donations from the first book, over $8,000 (and counting!) was raised and donated to the Children of Haiti Project. This exceeded our expectations and helped provide students with a full year of schooling, housing, a nutritional meal plan, vitamins, quarterly health checkups, vaccinations, uniforms, books, technology, and a core education in two languages. There has also been extensive teacher training and family programs provided that go beyond the school day to empower staff and families in the community.

As if that wasn't enough motivation, there were fellow international teachers from around the world who were eager to share their stories. Of the 40 authors in this second volume, 29 were not contributors to the first edition. Whether returning or new, they reminded us how powerful telling one's own story can be. These tales have a unique ability to serve as both windows and mirrors for each reader. Windows to view what life is like teaching and living in another country, and mirrors to reflect our humanity, how the experiences of joy, pain, good fortune, and loss are with us no matter where we go in the world.

Whether or not this second volume completes our "family" or inspires us to add another member is still to be determined. Regardless, the journey taken to curate each of *The New Normal* collections has been worth it. We hope you agree.

# CHILDREN OF HAITI PROJECT

100% of all proceeds from this book goes to support educating students via the Children of Haiti Project. To donate extra or to learn more, please go to http://www.childrenofhaitiproject.org/.

# INTERESTED IN SUBMITTING A STORY?

If you are interested in submitting a story for a potential third volume, please send your name and/or story to TheNewNormalBook@gmail.com.

# THANK YOUS

## FROM MATT:

It is both time-consuming and stressful to write a book. I truly can't think of many people I could work with so "closely" from 11,855 miles away. A huge thank you to Dunc for the Skype calls and laughter along the way. Sometimes those calls even managed to cover a little bit of book business.

I was a bit off of my game for a few months trying to meet book deadlines while balancing a job and my constant need to socialize. A very big thank you to my wife Cailin, one of the most self-aware introverts I know, for dealing with my extreme extroversion and constant need to talk about the writing process.

After our first book was published, I spent a lot of time thinking about how I grew to love reading and writing. Hours spent writing her own book, and carefully selecting young adult books for an immature, "jock" son was all part of Mom's long term plan. A special thanks to my mom for believing I could be a writer long before I ever did.

I debated for a while about whether or not to share the personal story of my dad's final few months before he passed. Some people may view that as a private time in our lives, but Dad loved a meaningful story, whether told by himself, a friend, or a stranger. A heartfelt thank you to my dad for showing me the importance of being an open book.

Growing up with selfless and supportive parents was always the norm in my childhood and adulthood. Watching my brother now follow in our parents' footsteps while parenting his own two boys is inspiring. Although we have chosen very different paths in life, I always feel his love and support regardless of where life leads me. A huge "Brothers Don't Shake Hands, Brothers Gotta" hug, and thank you to my brother Mikey for picking up where Dad left off.


FROM KEVIN:

I can think of hundreds, if not thousands, of people I would rather work with from 11,855 miles away, but I somehow got stuck with Matty O'Minor. I'm sure it could be worse though. Not sure how, but I guess it could.

Seriously, though, a big thank you to Matt. Your organization, advice (on book items and on life), critiques, communication, willingness to do so many tedious but necessary tasks, and overall dedication to this project were invaluable from start to finish. Also, thank you for inspiring me by wholly embracing your #thisis40 challenge on the art of storytelling.

For being there when I needed advice on my own story and for providing support and helpful feedback throughout the entire process, my sincerest thanks to Lindsay.

My love of reading began at an early age, before I even have distinct memories. My mom and dad read to me as an infant, encouraged me to read as a child, and went above and beyond in their support of my education. They exemplified how important it was to keep learning, long after our formal education ended. My parents continued to learn new skills such as making stained glass or how to run a meeting using parliamentary procedure, even after all their kids had left the house. Though my dad has passed since the first book was published, the impact he made on his children, grandchildren, and so many others will continue to live on. Mom and Dad—I can't thank you enough.

FROM BOTH OF US:

Thank you to Bambi Betts and TIE Online for continuing to partner with us to support the Children of Haiti Project. Your generous contribution allowed us to secure a very talented editing team.

Thank you to Ken and Kathy Turner for your tremendous editing work. Your valuable insights regarding how to make stories better helped so many of us authors reach our potential. You provided high quality analysis at multiple phases of the story improvement process that was both thorough and timely. This collection greatly benefitted from your generosity and wisdom.

Thank you to Matt Smith for sharing your artistic skills on the front and back cover and for finding ways to meet deadlines in between traveling to gigs around the world that actually pay. Your attention to detail and willingness to adjust the cover several times was greatly appreciated. (For more information about Matt Smith and his workshops, check out his bio page at the end of this book or his website SmithvsSmith.com.)

Thank you to David Koellein for being our first set of eyes to look at the printed edition of volumes one and two in order to ensure that everything looked ready for release to the public.

Thank you to Matthew Dicks. In spite of the fact that neither of us have met you, by sharing your insightful storytelling advice and reaffirming the power of stories on Mike Pesca's and your own podcasts, we see the benefit of "Homework for Life" and understand how the smallest moments can often contain the biggest insights.

Thank you to the Story Selection Committee members who read and ranked potential stories. Your timeliness and thoughtful feedback helped make the selection process fair and efficient.

Thanks to Amy Anstey, Marie Beaupre, Danielle Bedard, Chelsea Bowen, Emerald Garvey, Jay Goodman, Tom Greenwood, Allen Koshewa, Crystal Lang, Bick McSwiney, Laura Mooberry, Jim Murphy, Natalie Murphy, Jen Tustin Park, Shannon Tustin Park, Susan Richey, Alicia Ritter, Lindsay Rude, Mama Sandz, and Michelle Westholm.

Thank you to our authors, who continue to model the importance of risk-taking. It is a vulnerable feeling to submit a story to be critiqued and picked apart. You handled that process with grace and showed the same humility and open-mindedness during the editing process that we hope and expect from our students.

Lastly, thank you to the readers and supporters whose feedback and excitement from the first volume led to this second one. We hope you connected with these stories, whether you live down the street from your childhood home or thousands of miles away. Most of all, thank you for supporting the Children of Haiti Project.

# ABOUT THE COVER ARTIST

Matt Smith is a British/Canadian cartoonist, filmmaker and educator. A true third culture kid, Matt attended the International School Bangkok and the International School of Kuala Lumpur, where he graduated with the IB Diploma. As an international teacher, Matt has taught all over the world in schools like the American School in Japan and the American International School Kuwait.

As a cartoonist, Matt is best known for his humorous autobiographical *Smith vs Smith* series. These comics about travel, marriage and cats, can be found online at SmithvsSmith.com and various strips have been published by *Sliced Quarterly* and the University of Victoria's *Martlet* newspaper. Stories from Matt's horror series, *Gruesome Comics*, in which he teams up with a variety of international artists, have been published by *Alterna Comics*, *Soaring Penguin Press* and *Hangman Comics*.

These days, Matt's focus is on comics education. He travels across the world to schools like the International Community School of Addis Ababa, the American Community School of Abu Dhabi and Munich International School, helping students from kindergarten to Grade 12 to create their own comics. He has brought his lessons to English classes, art classes, business classes and even German classes. Matt's core belief is that ANYone can draw comics, regardless of artistic background.

Matt also facilitates professional development sessions for teachers, where he demonstrates the sophistication and literary-value of comics, equipping teachers with the knowledge needed to bring comics into their classrooms. In March 2019, Matt was a workshop presenter at the EARCOS (East Asia Regional Council of Schools) conference held at his alma mater, the International School Bangkok.

If you or your school are interested in Matt's interactive, engaging comics-making workshops, you can find more information at SmithvsSmith.com/workshops-lessons, contact Matt by email at Matt@SmithvsSmith.com, or reach out on social media.

SmithvsSmith.com
@smithvssmithcomics on Instagram & Facebook
@smithvssmith on Twitter